MOUSE
COLORING BOOK

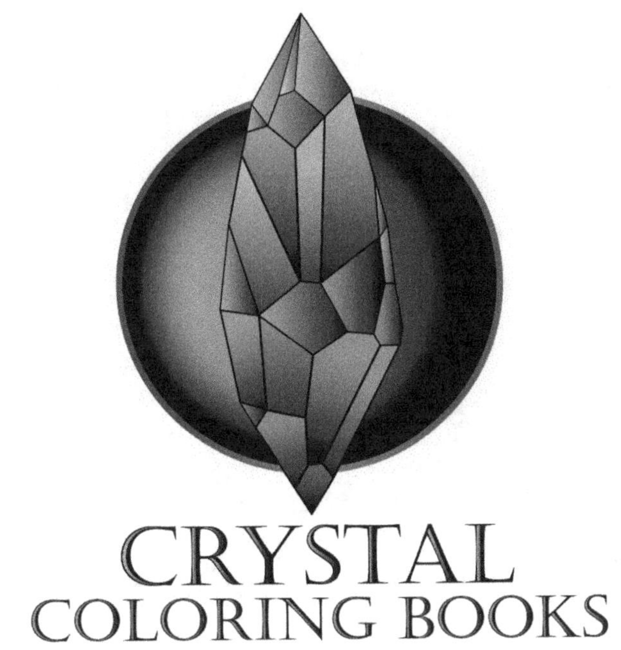

CRYSTAL
COLORING BOOKS

Copyright © 2017 Crystal Coloring Books
All rights reserved.

ISBN-13: 978-1986007443
ISBN-10: 1986007448

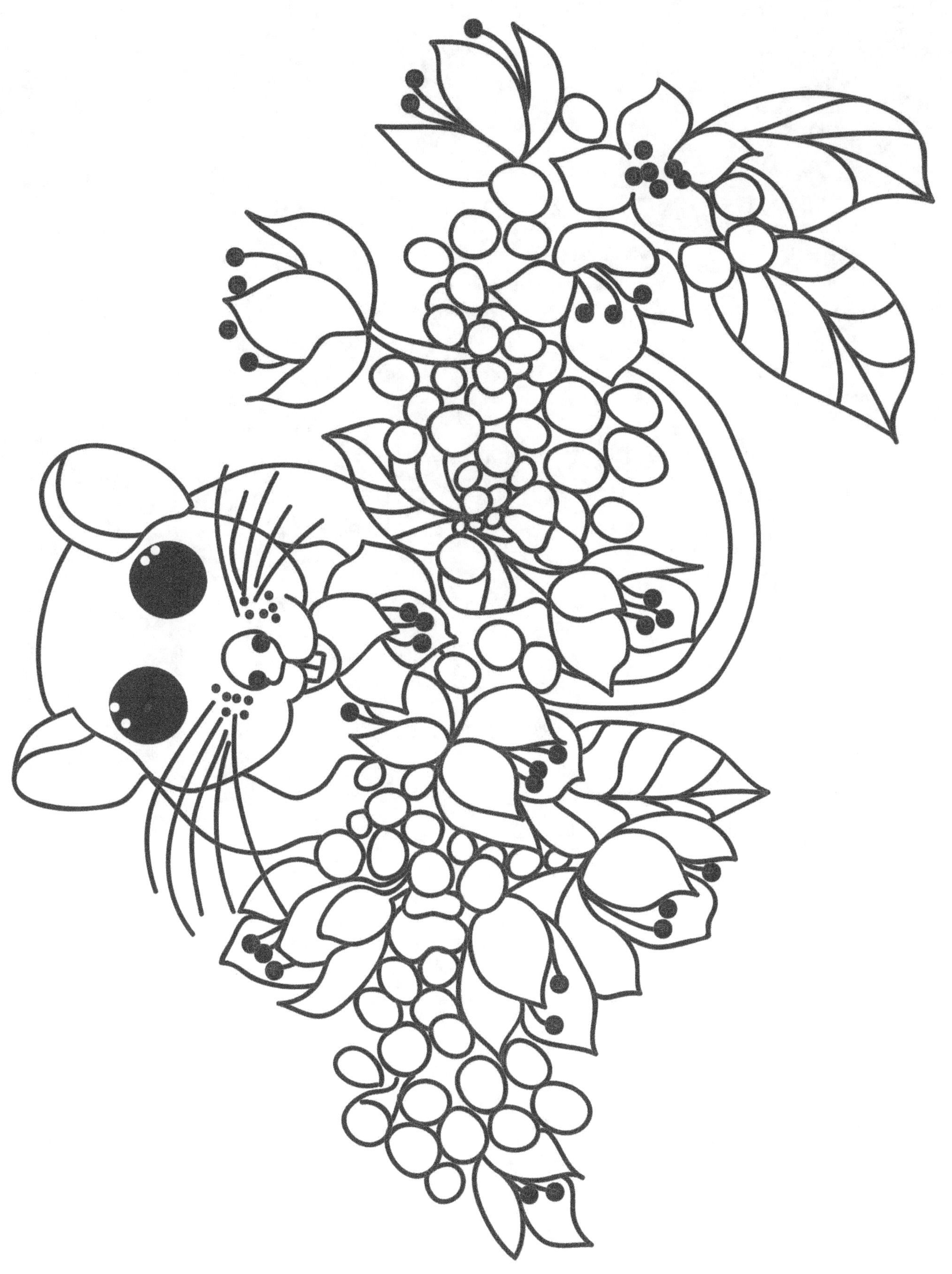

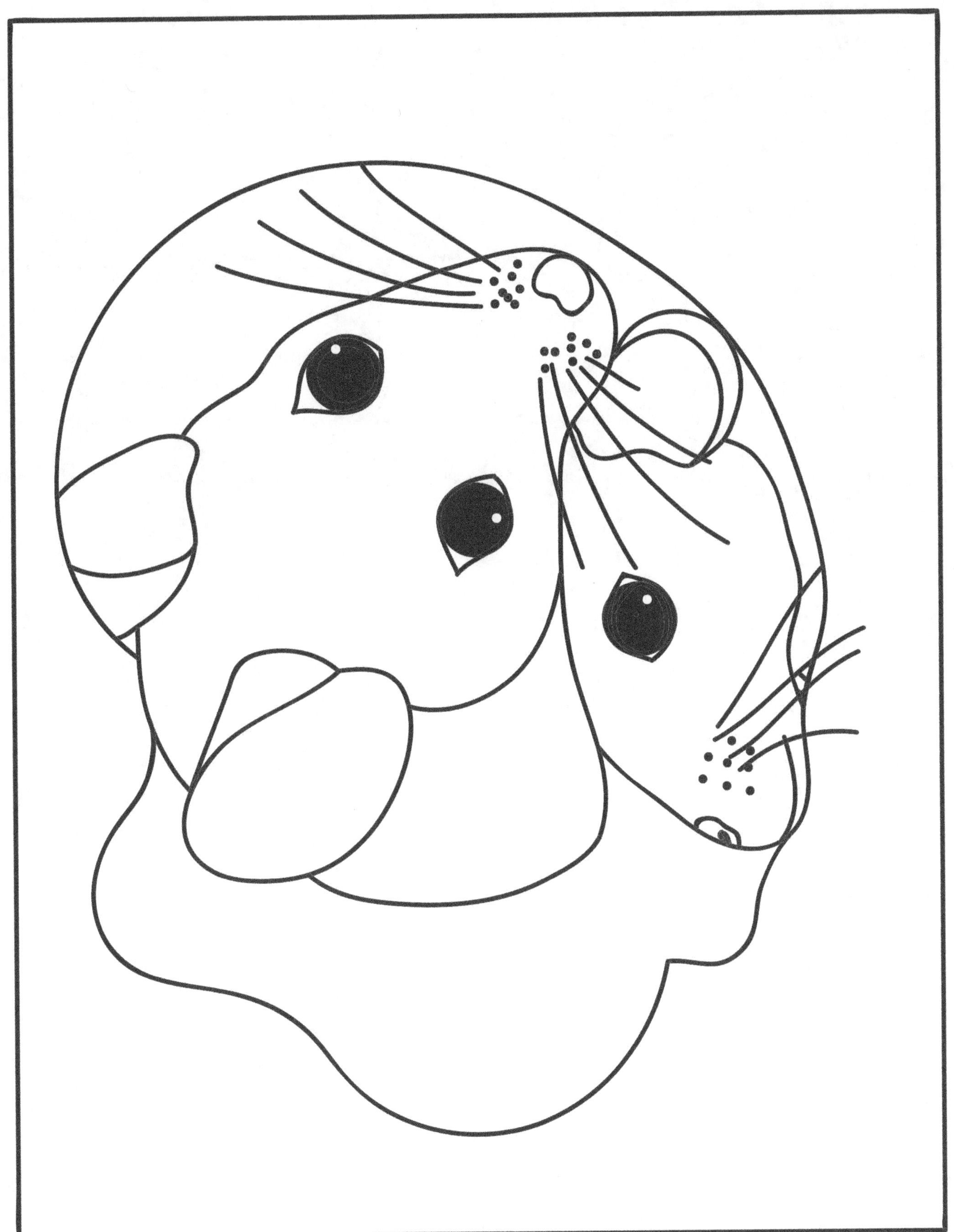

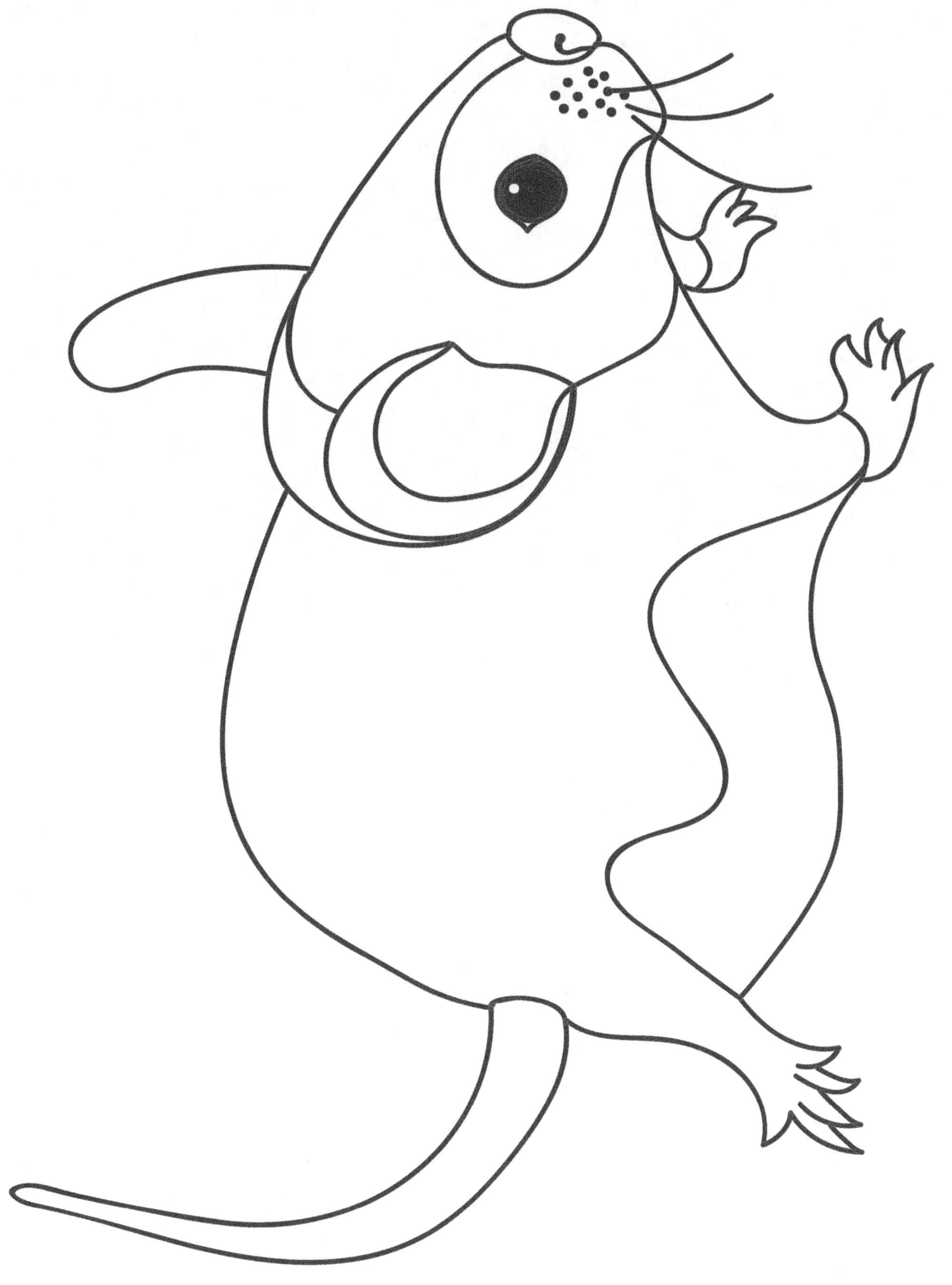

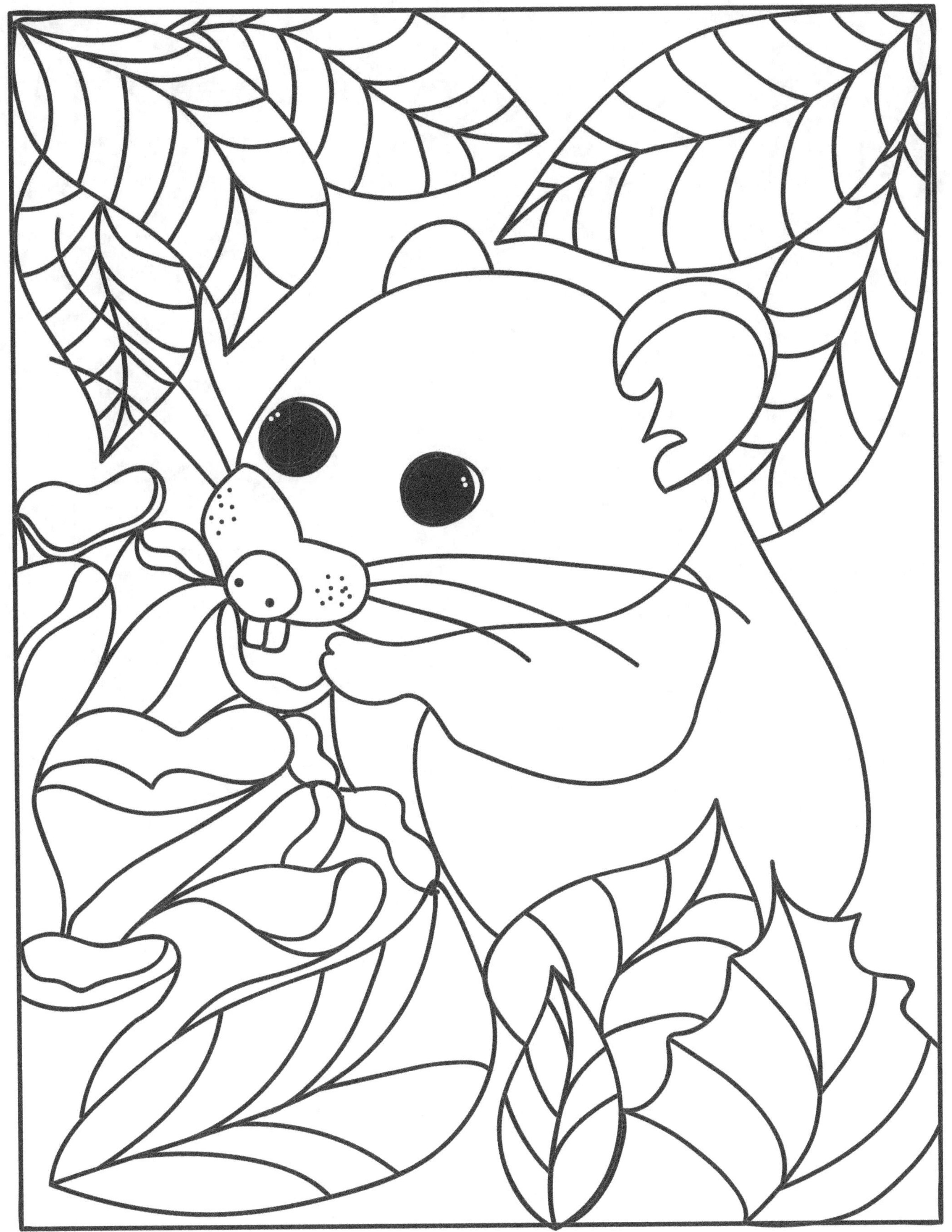

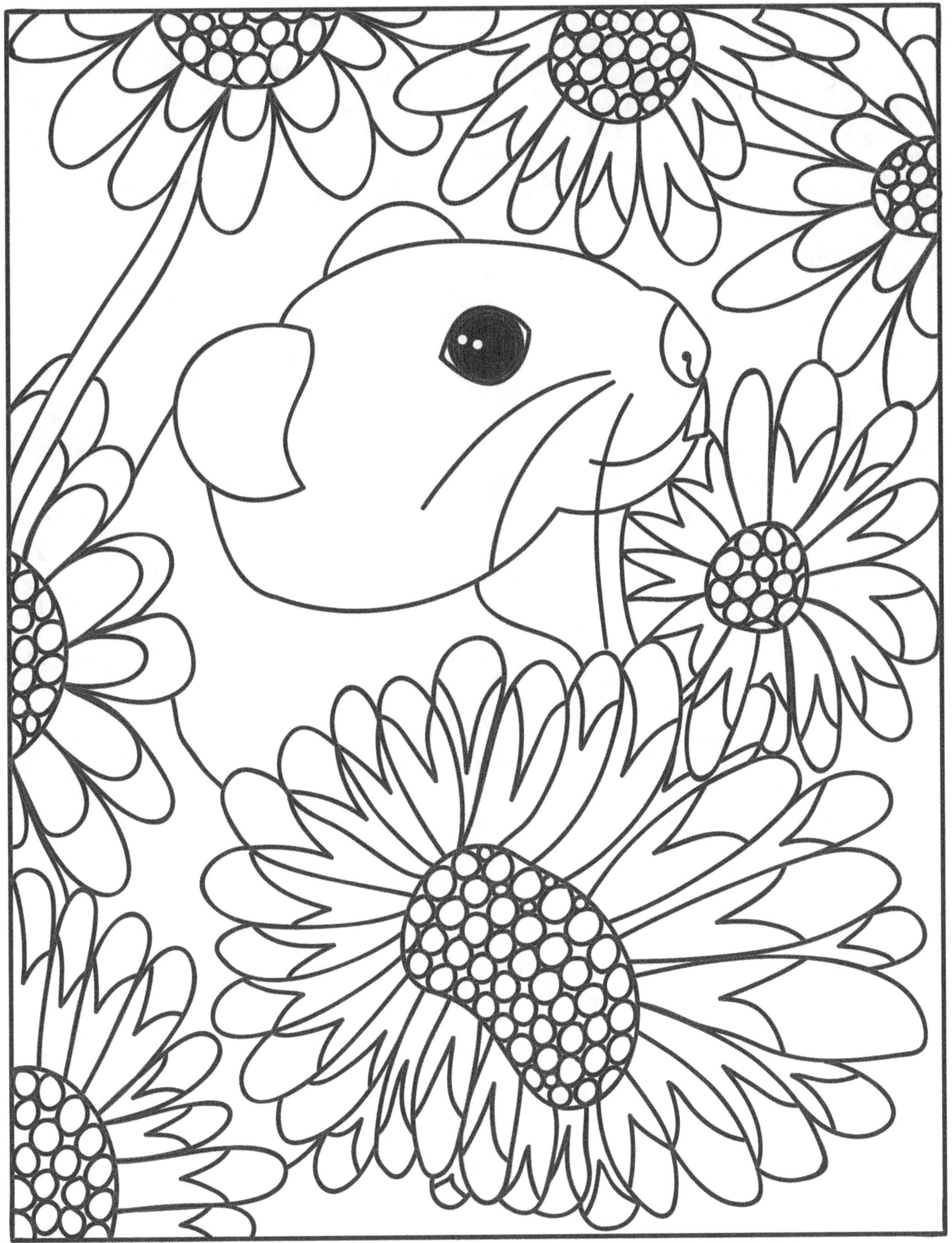

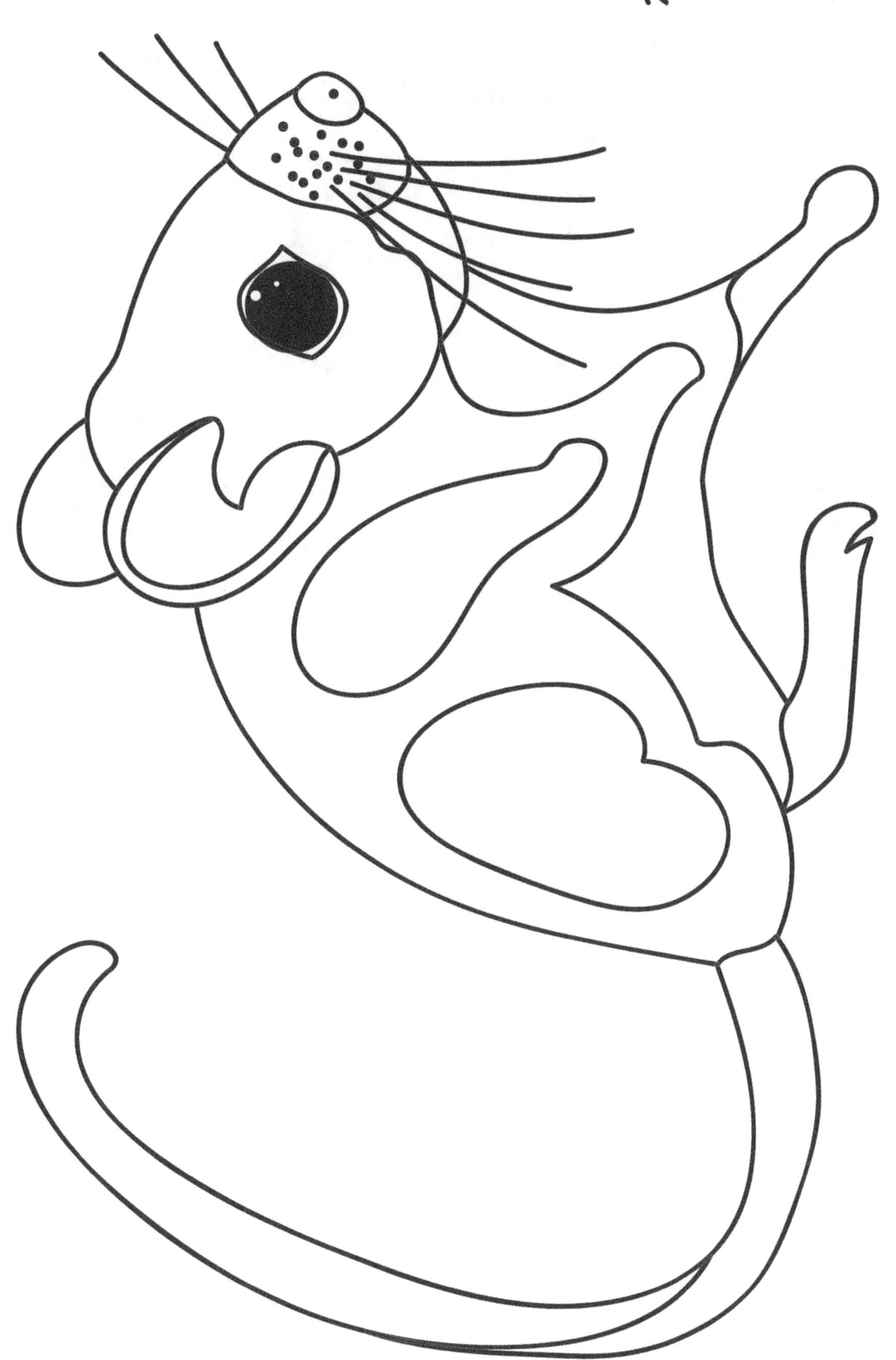

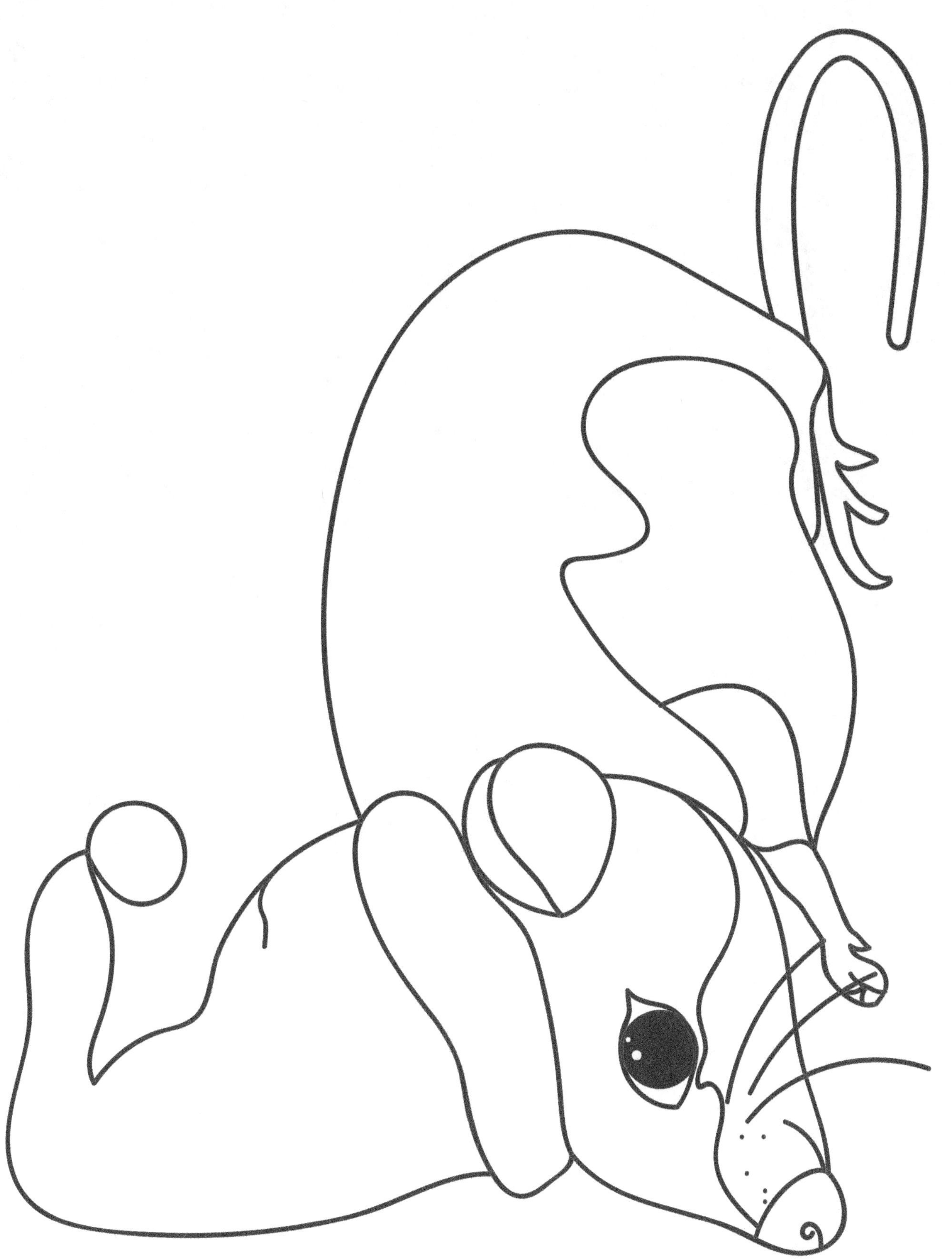

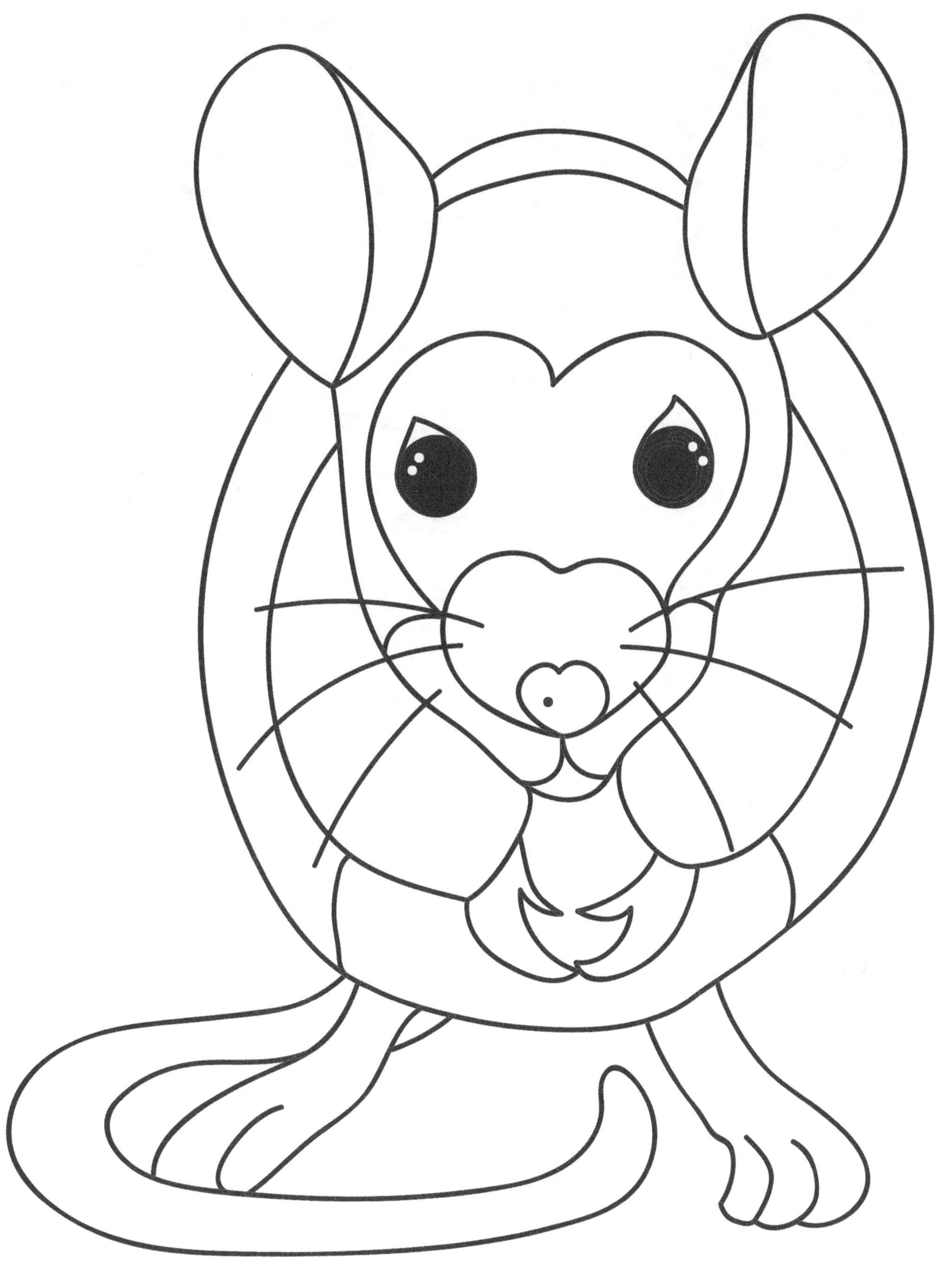

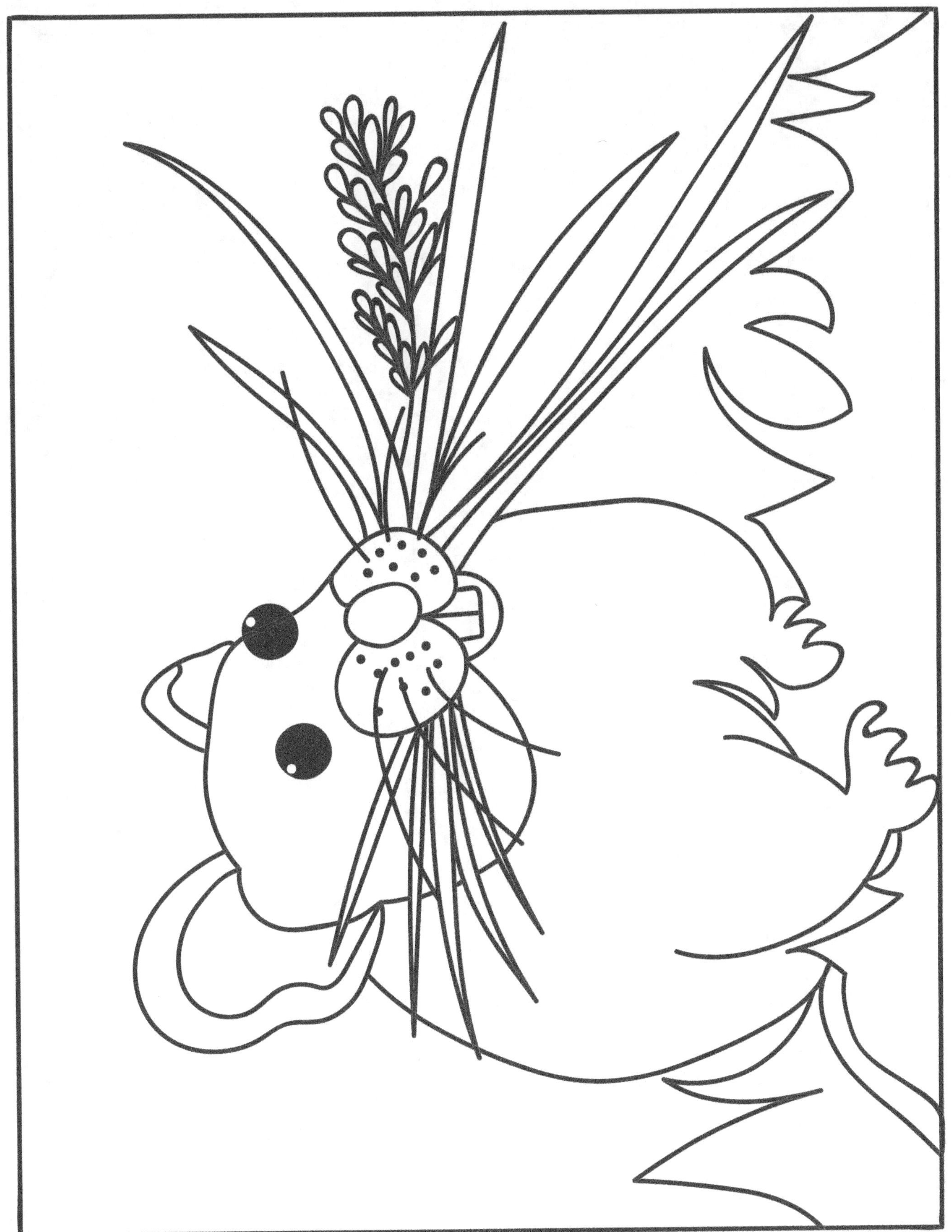

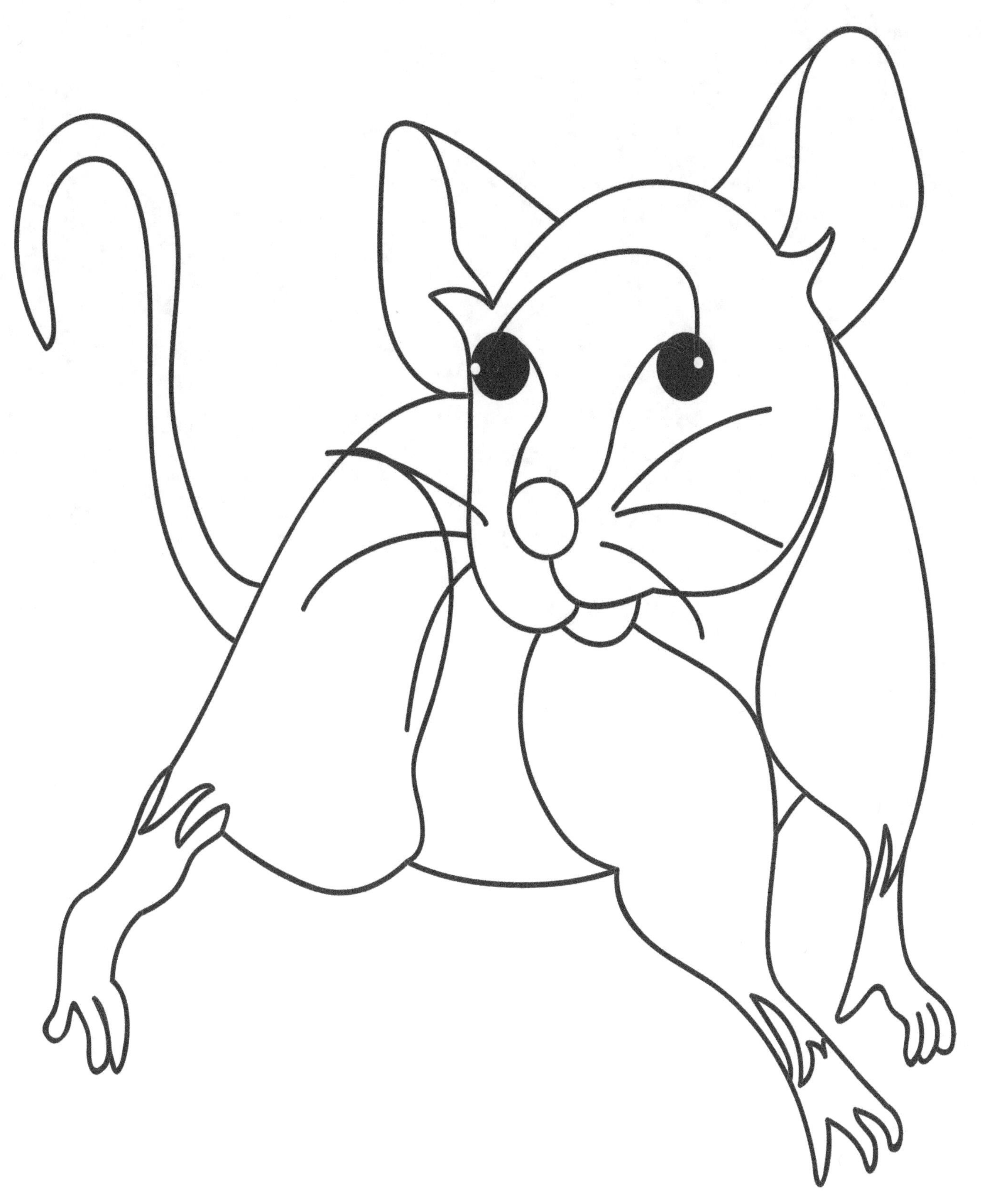

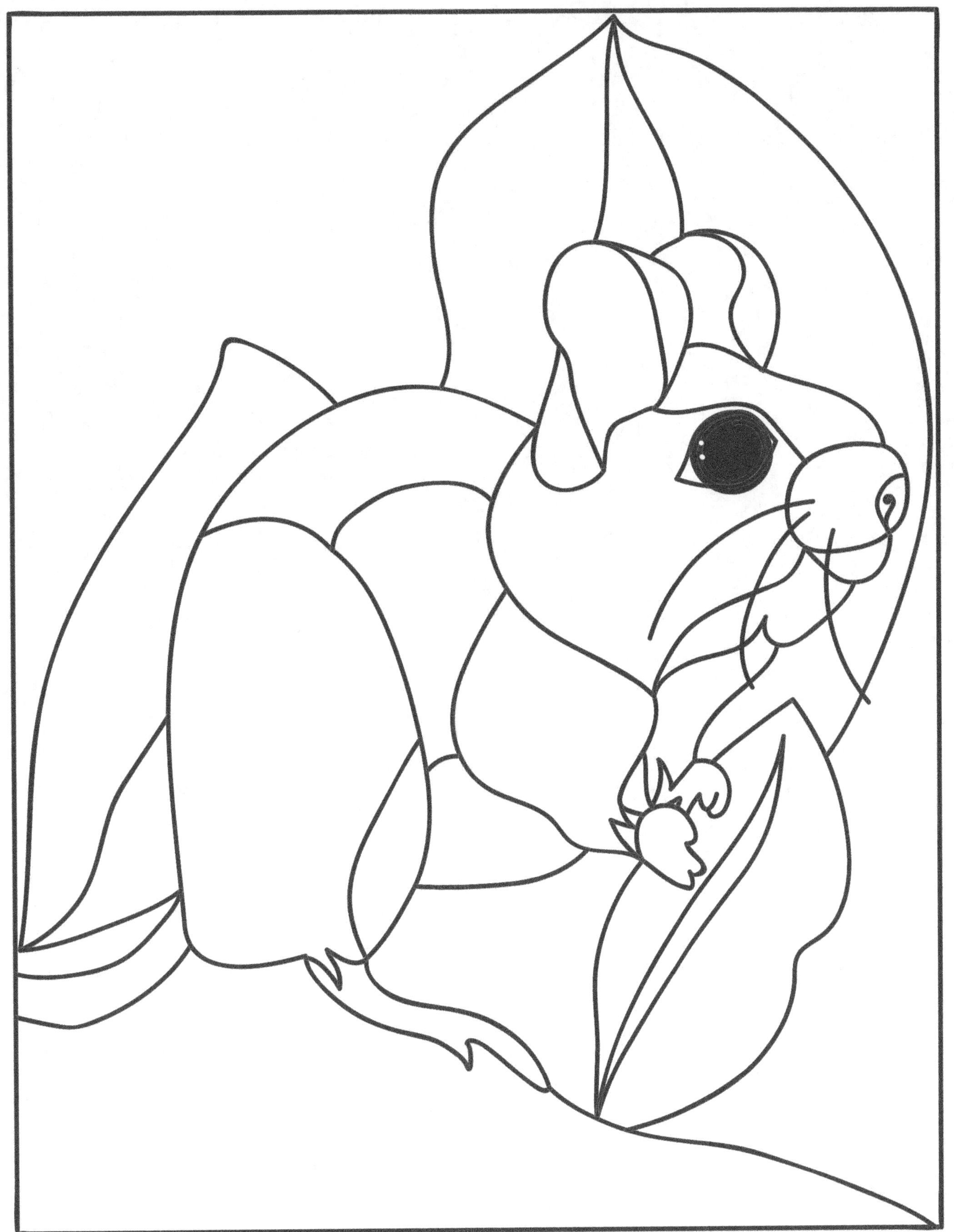

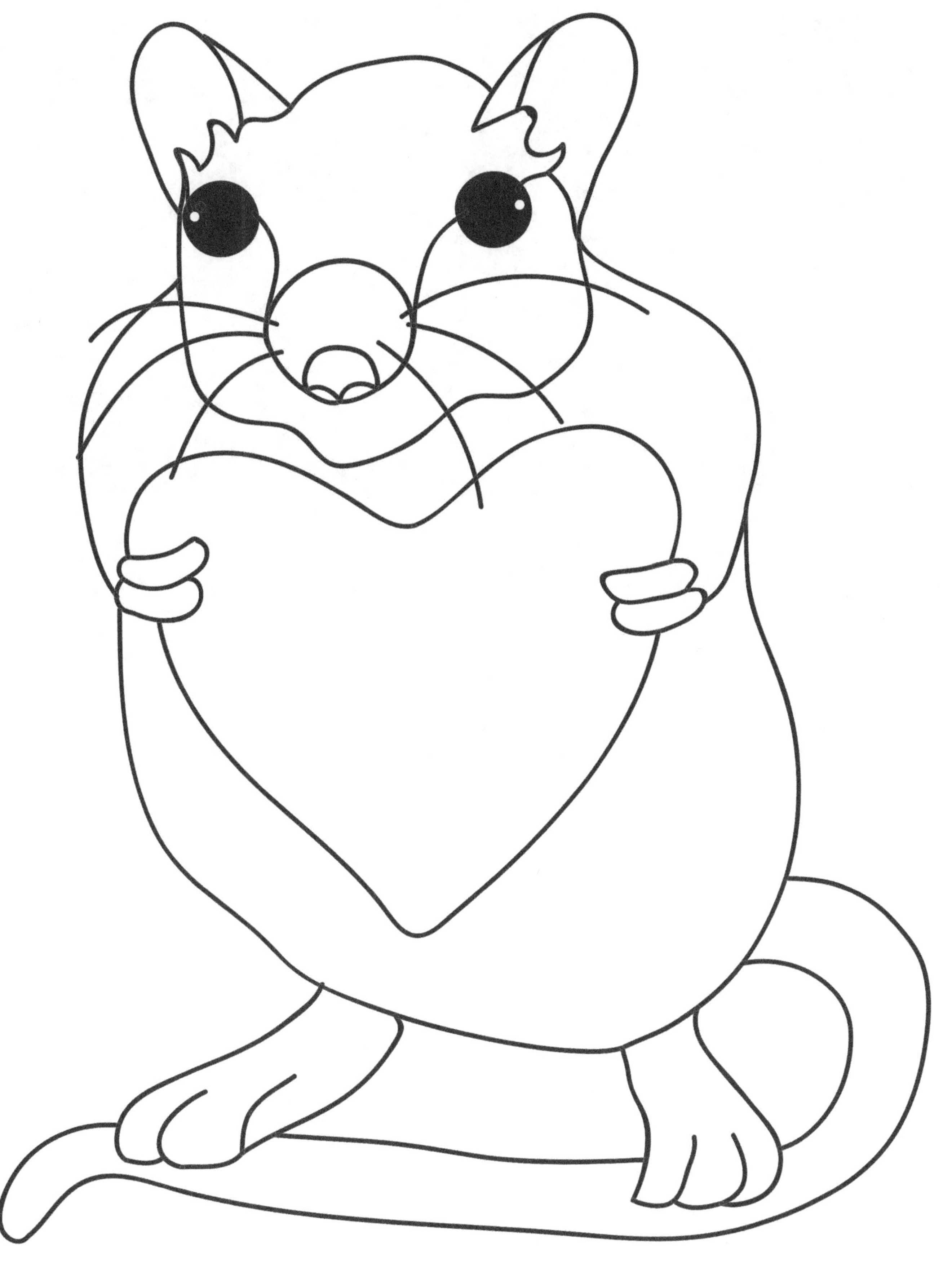

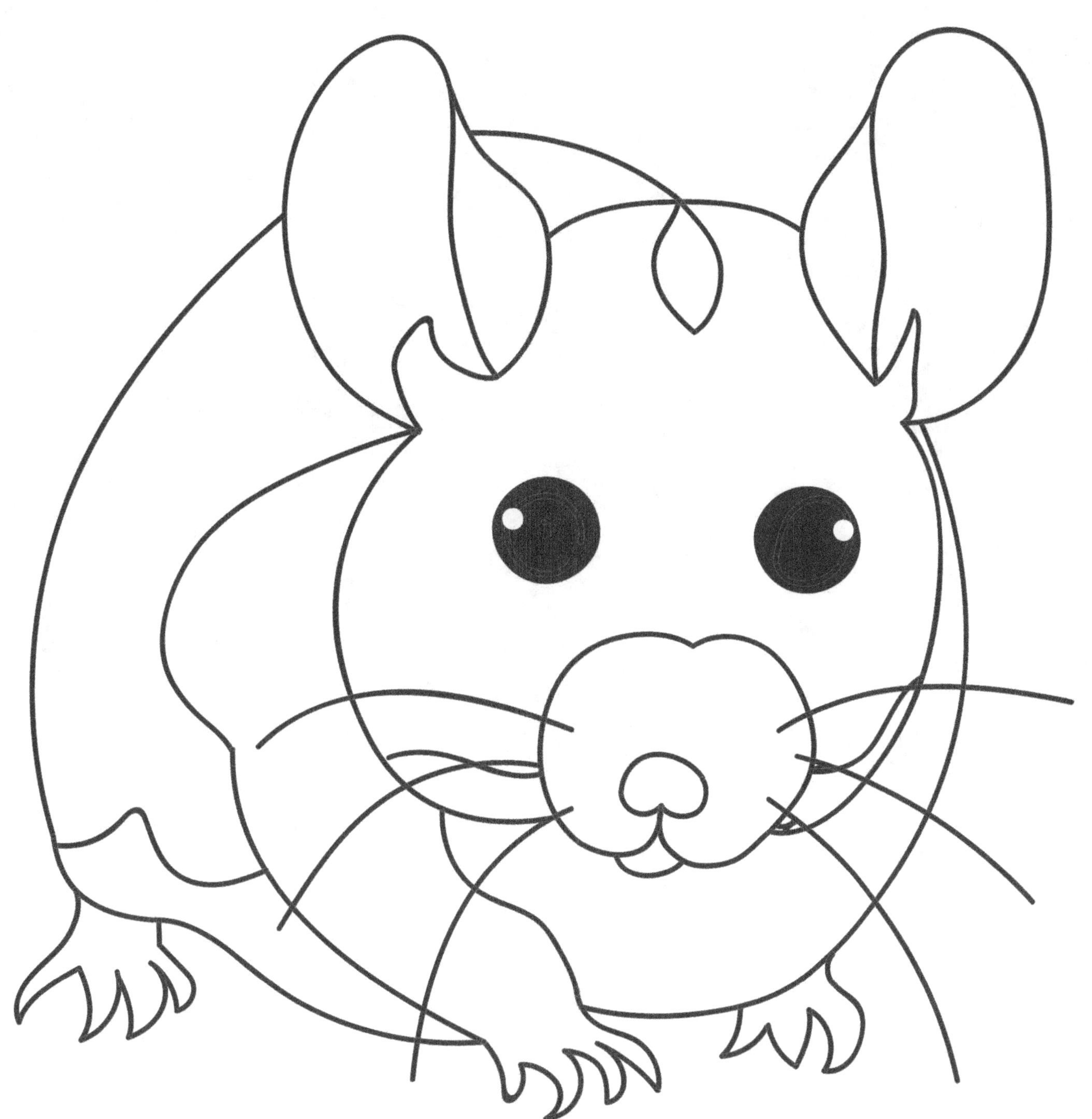

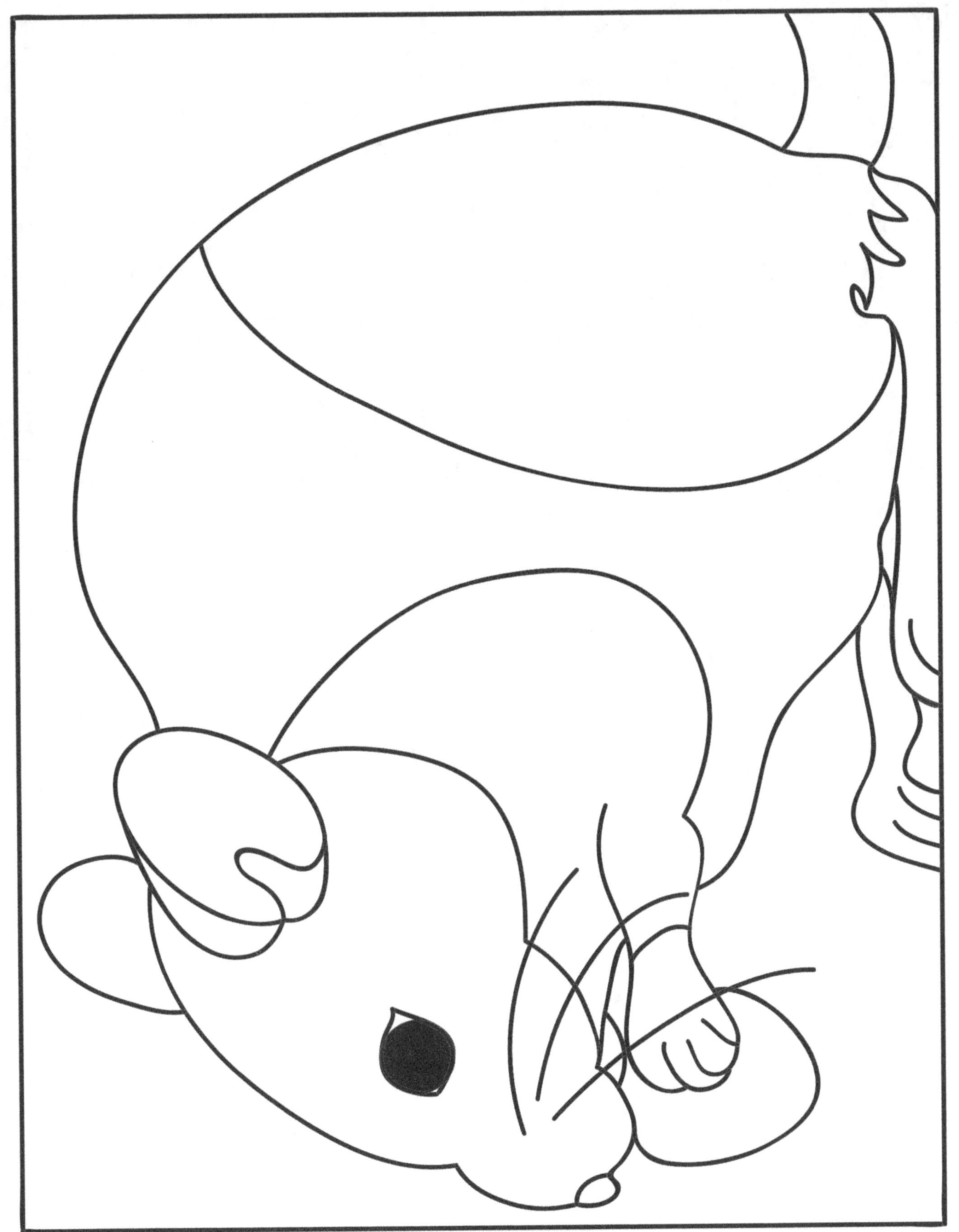

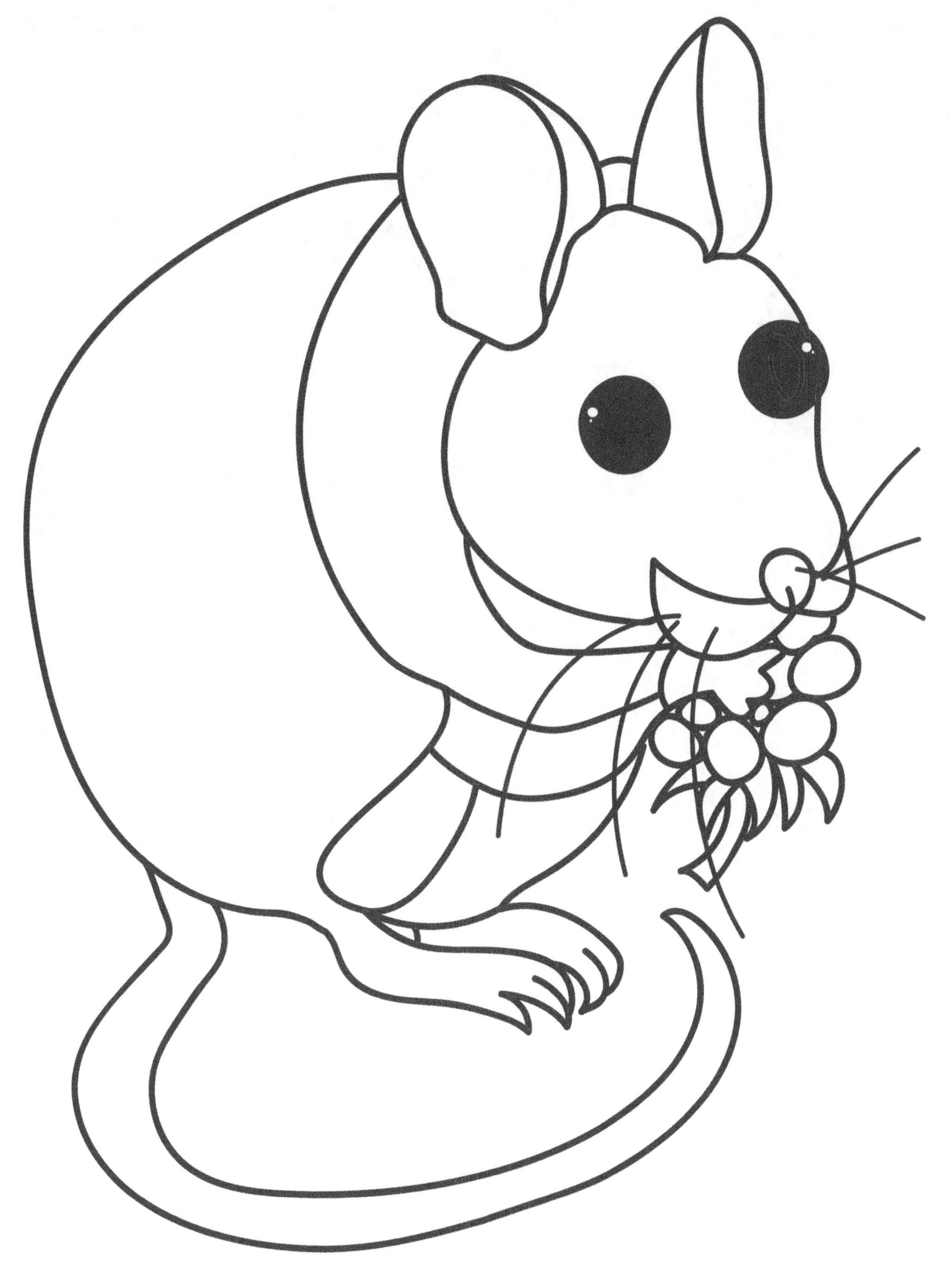

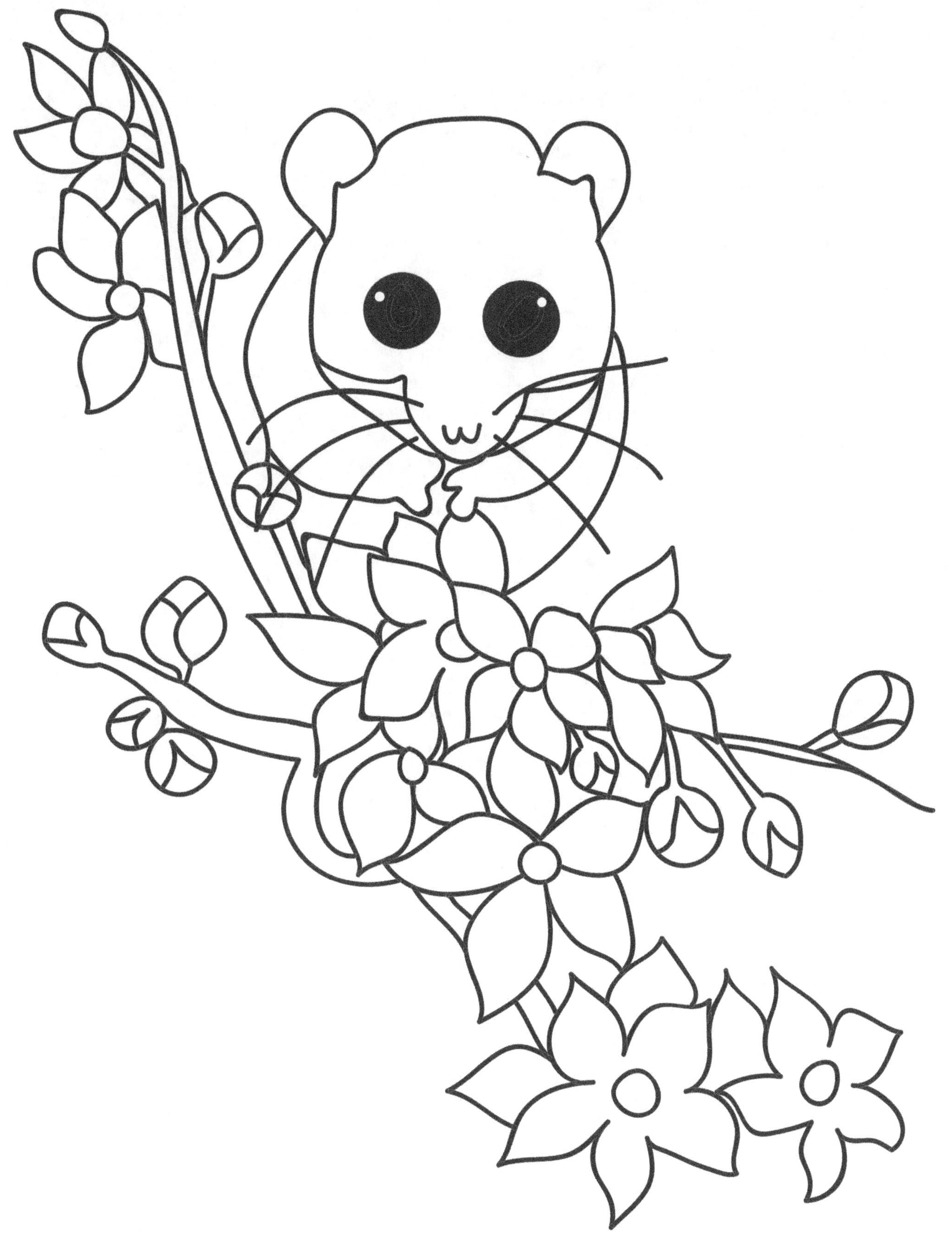

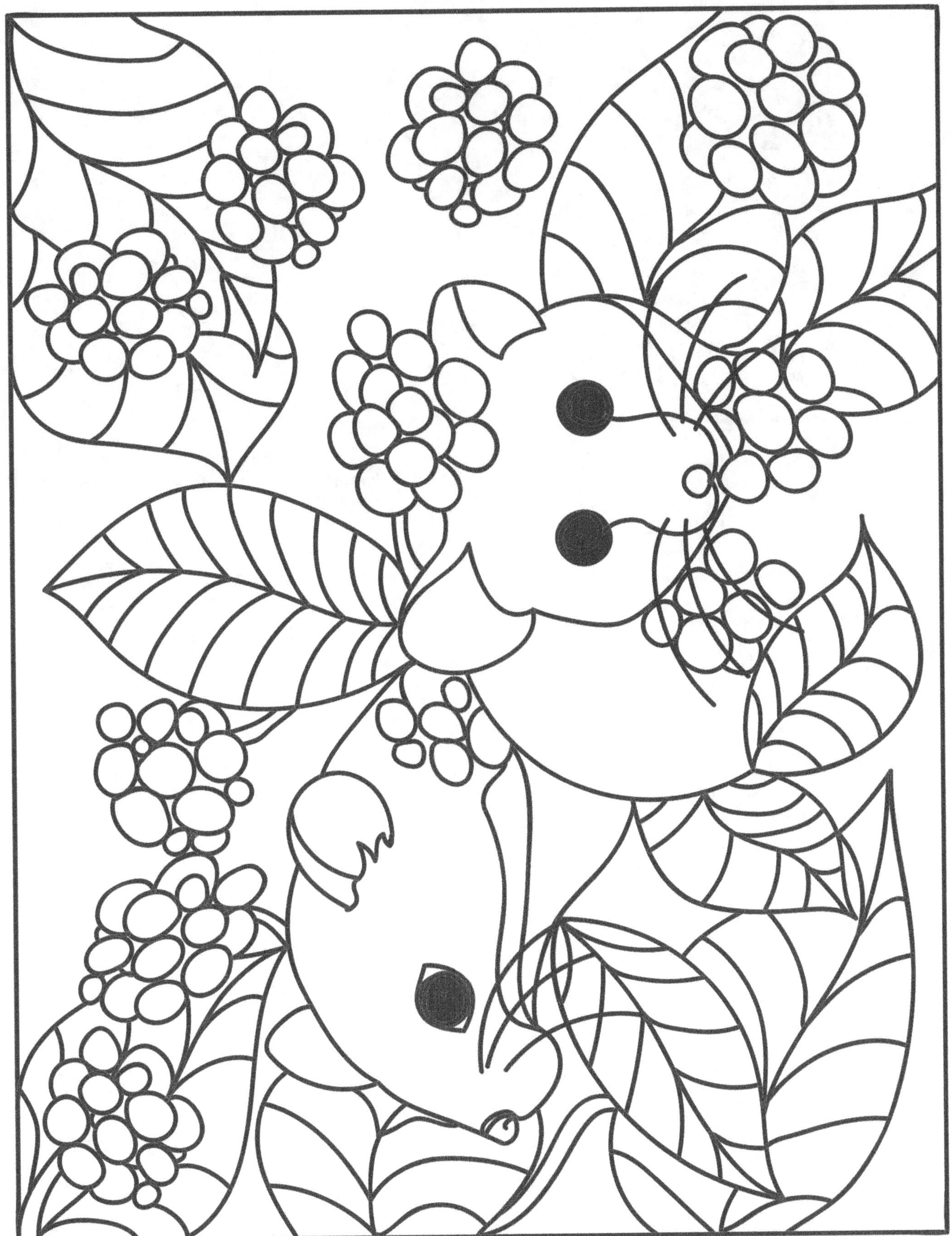

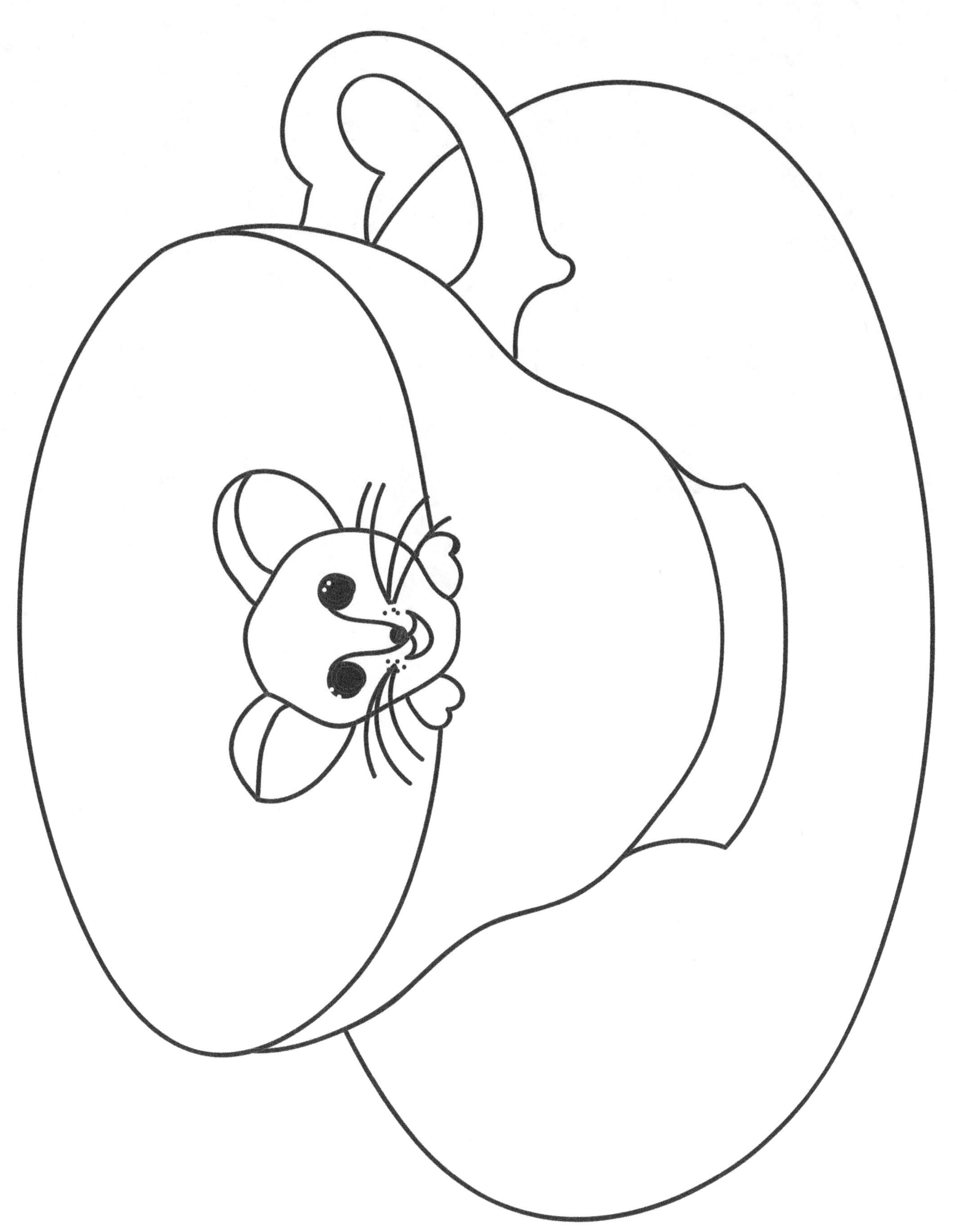

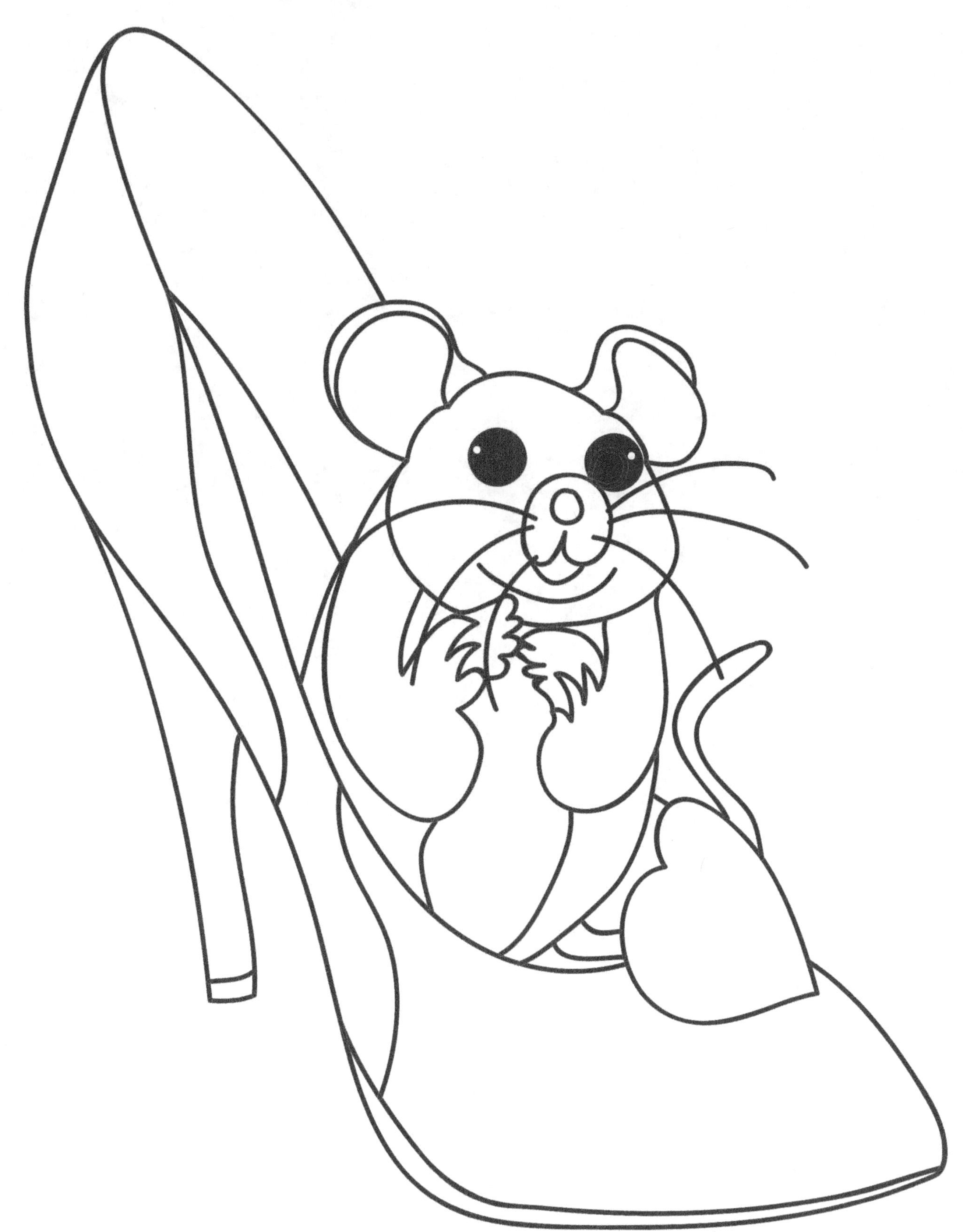

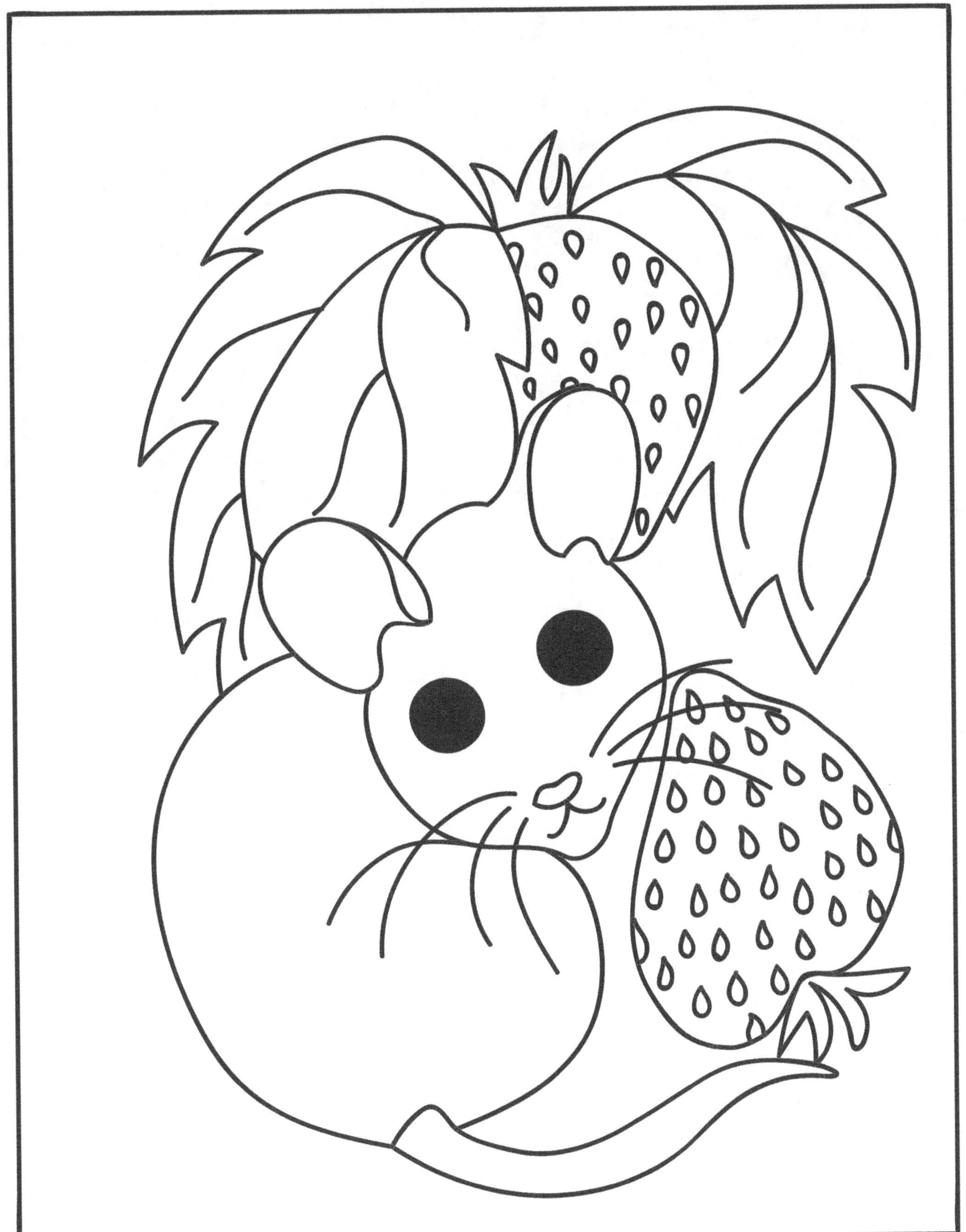

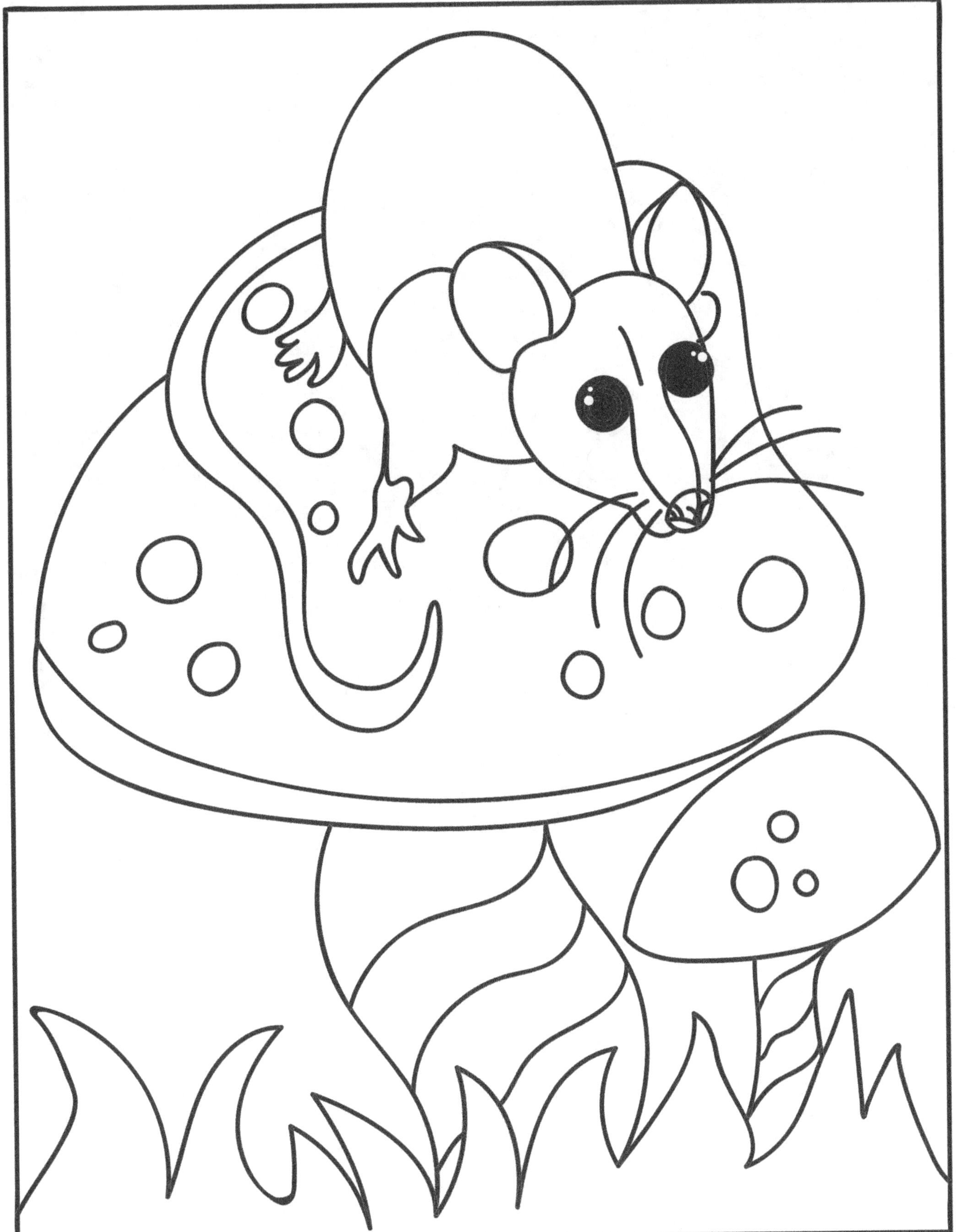

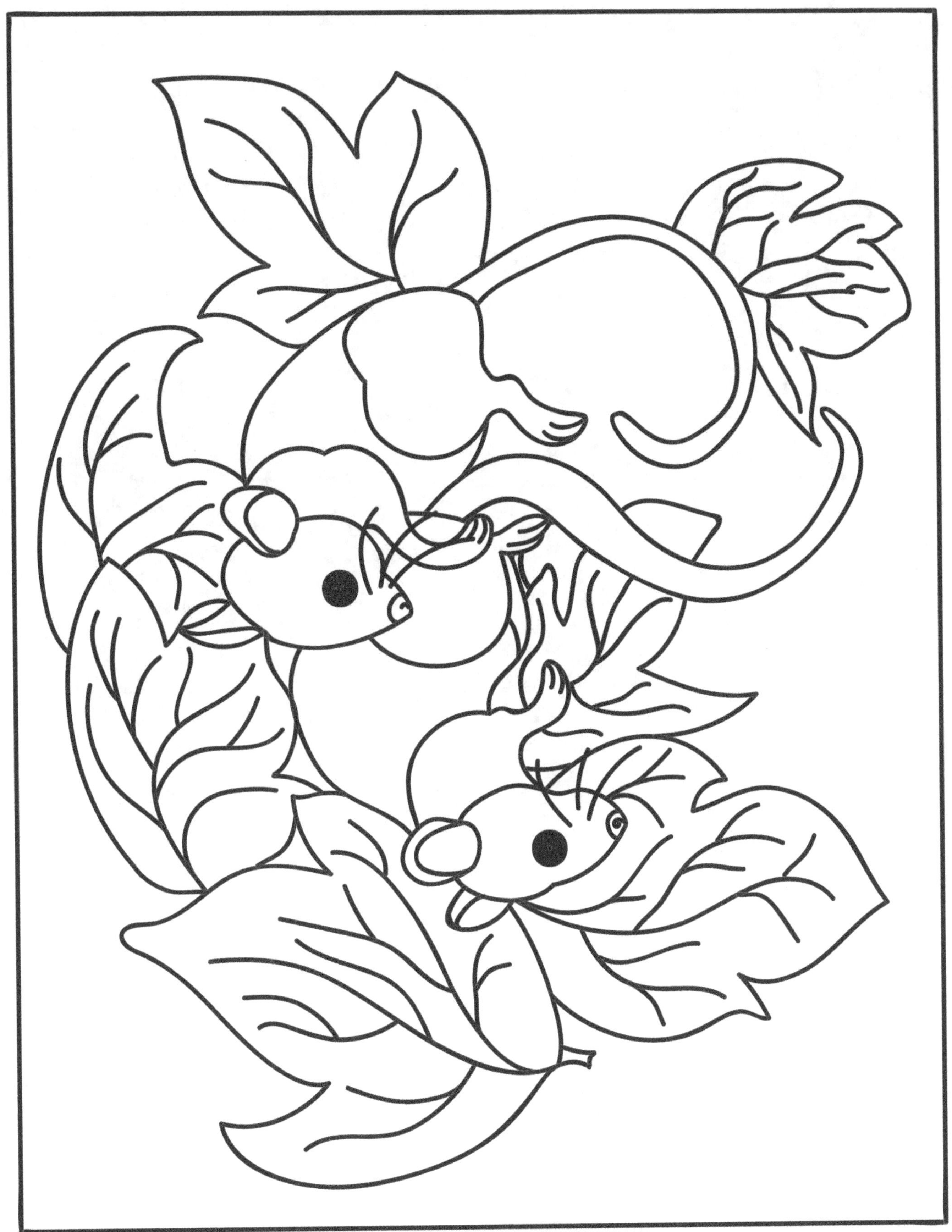

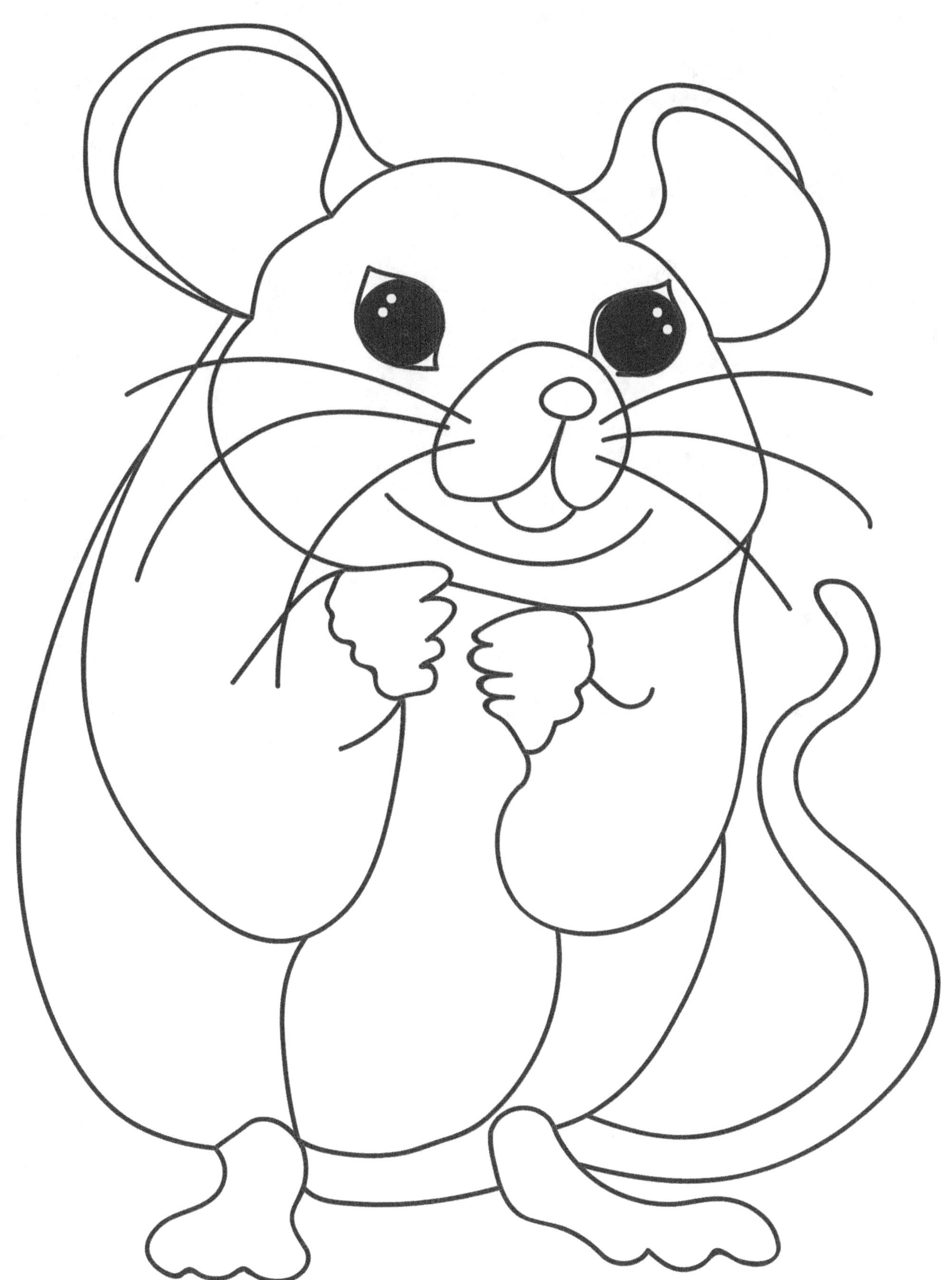

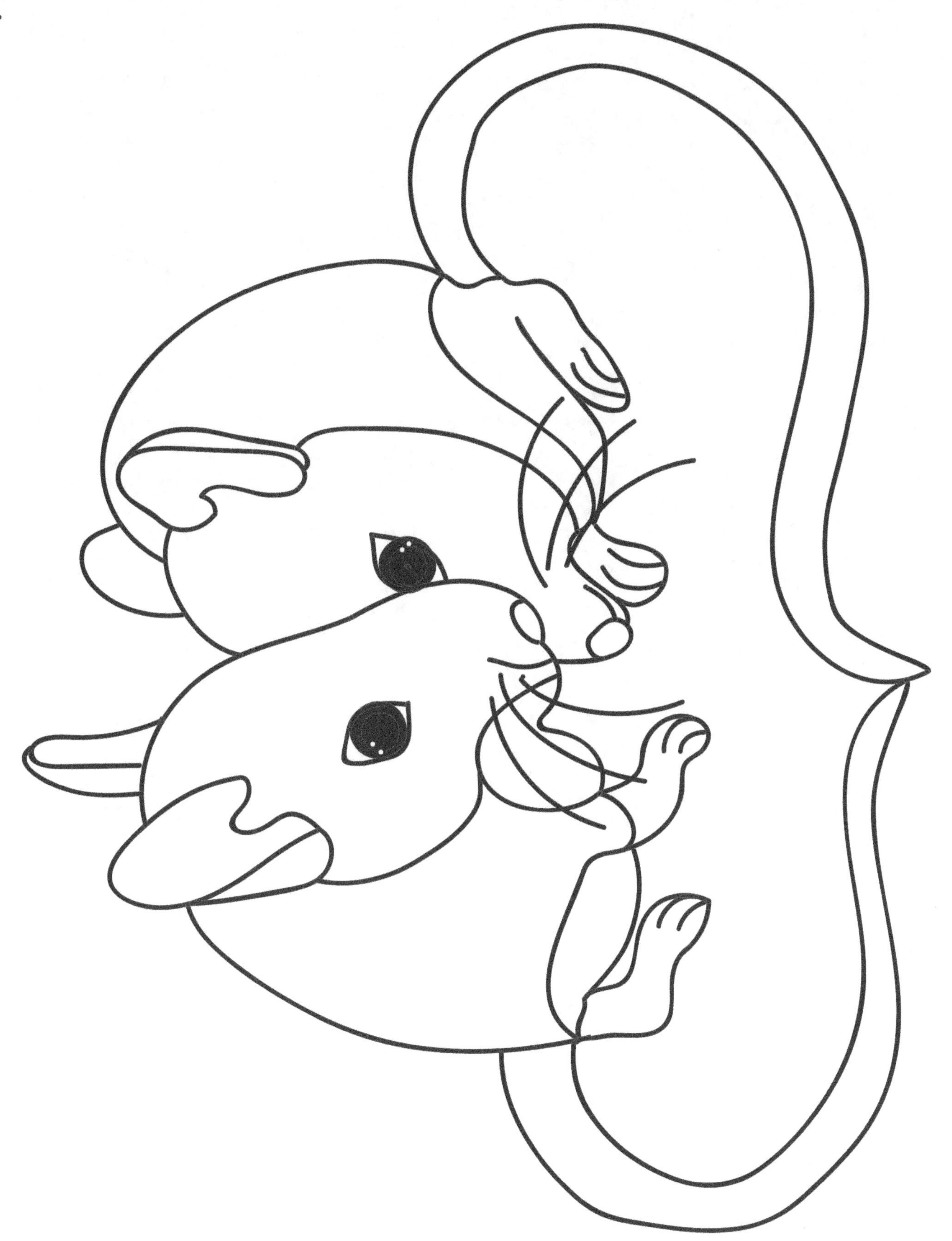

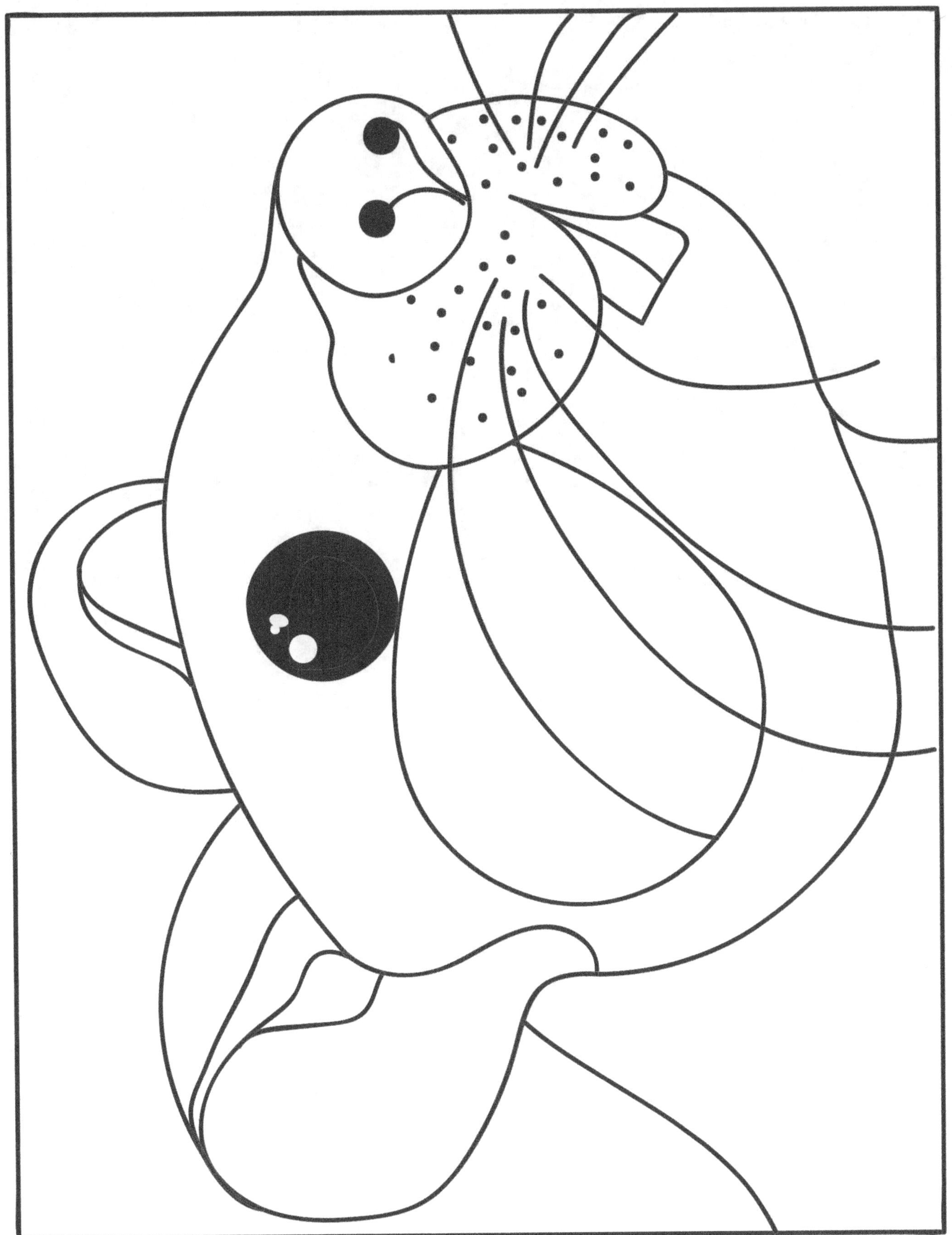

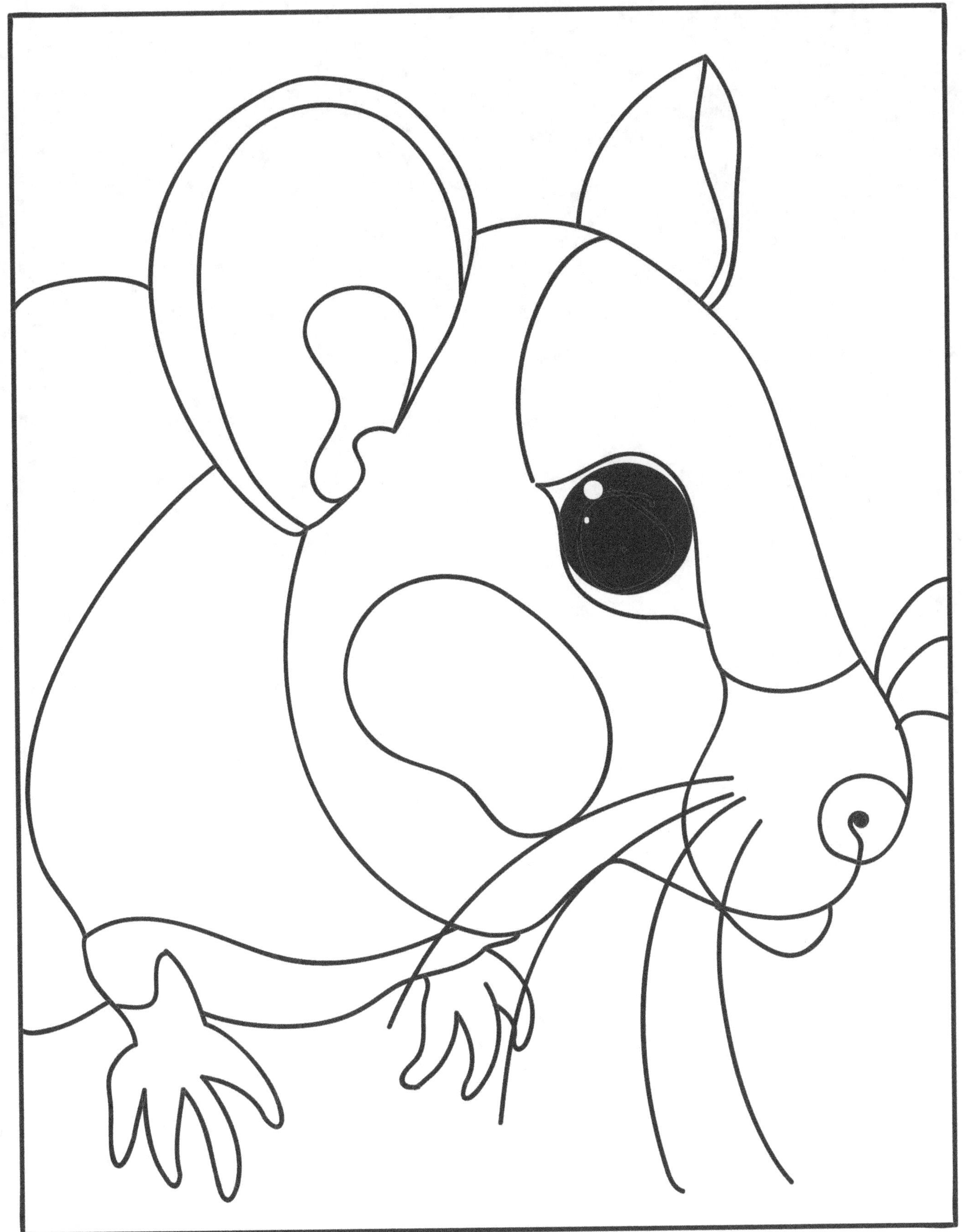

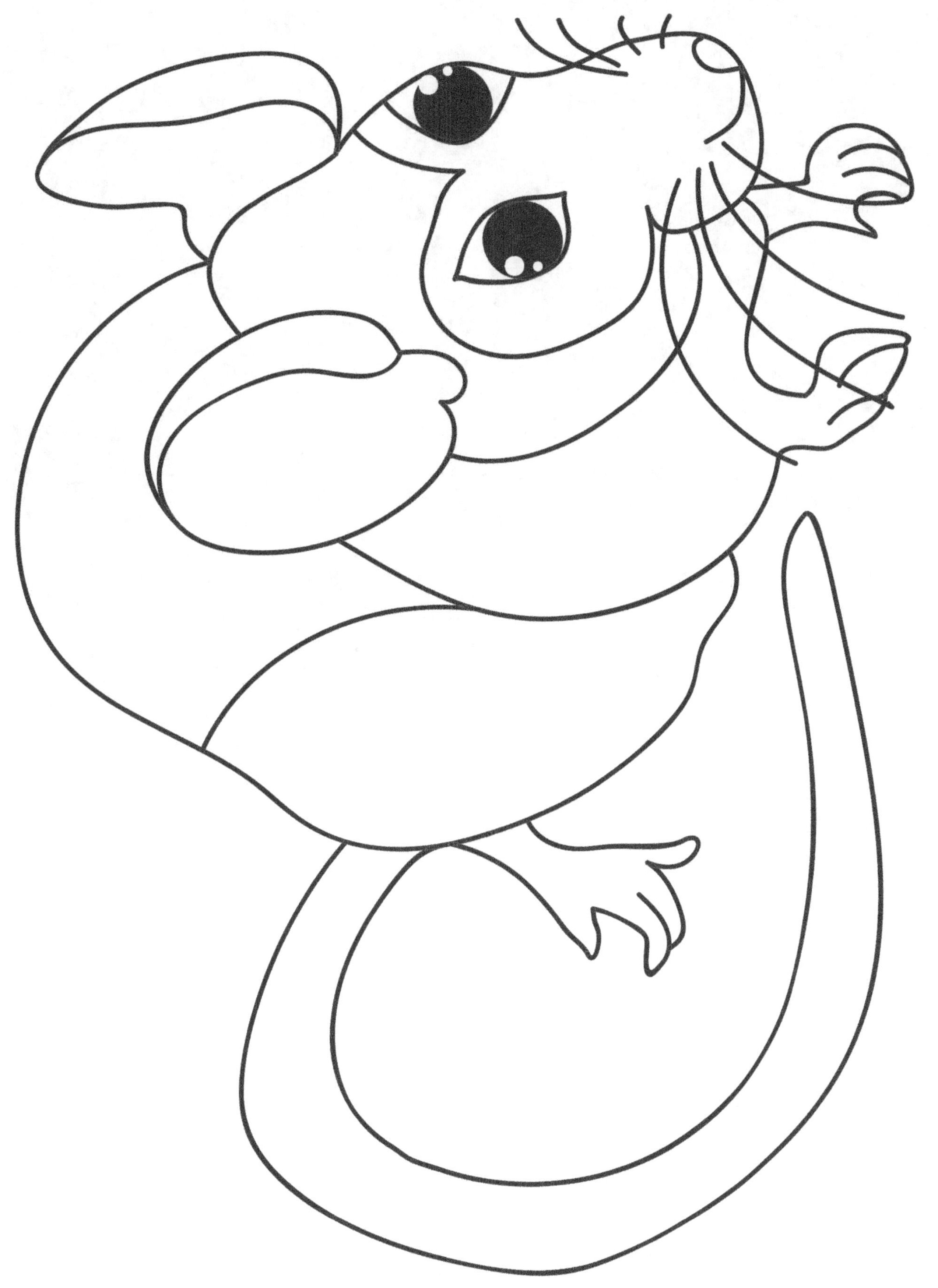

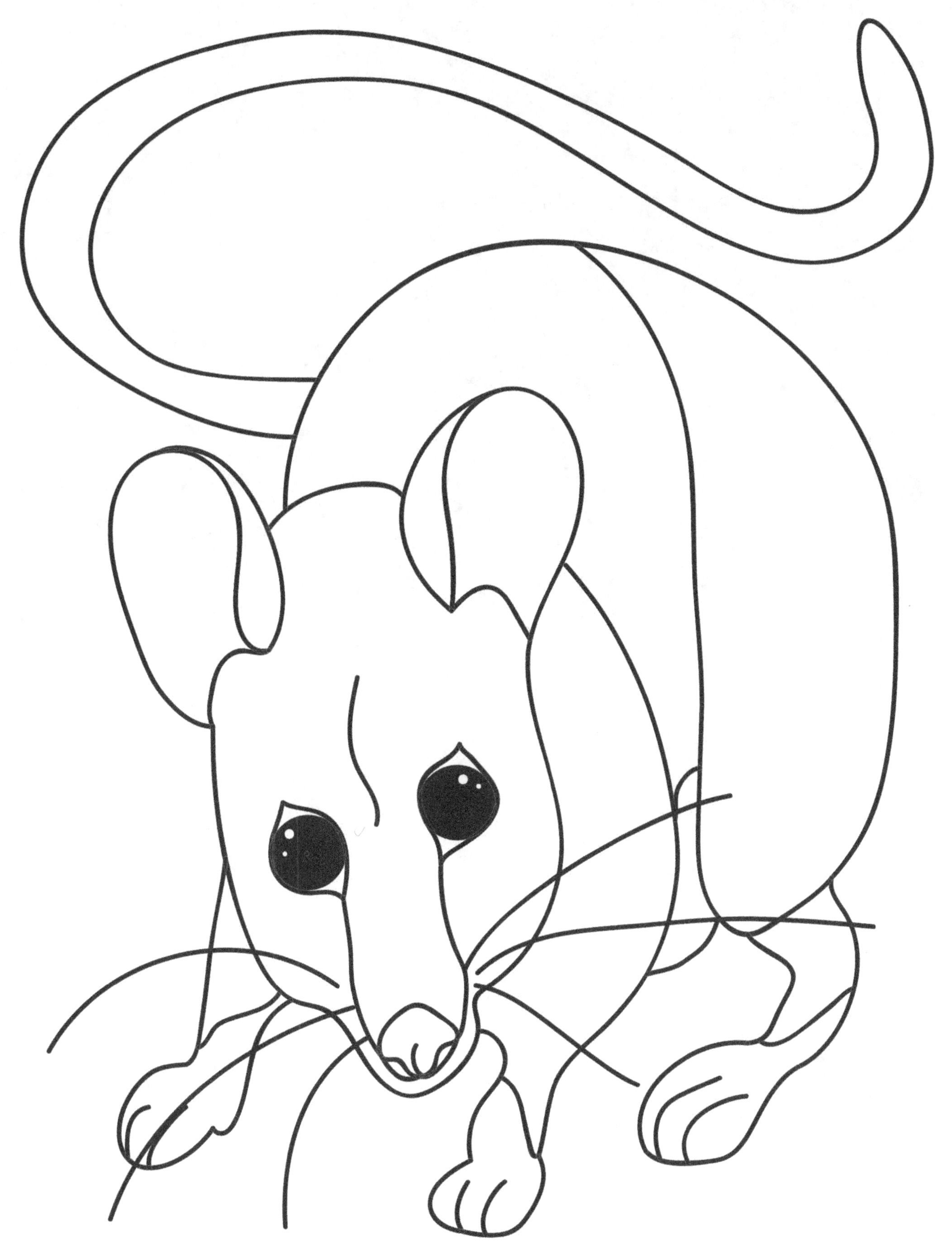

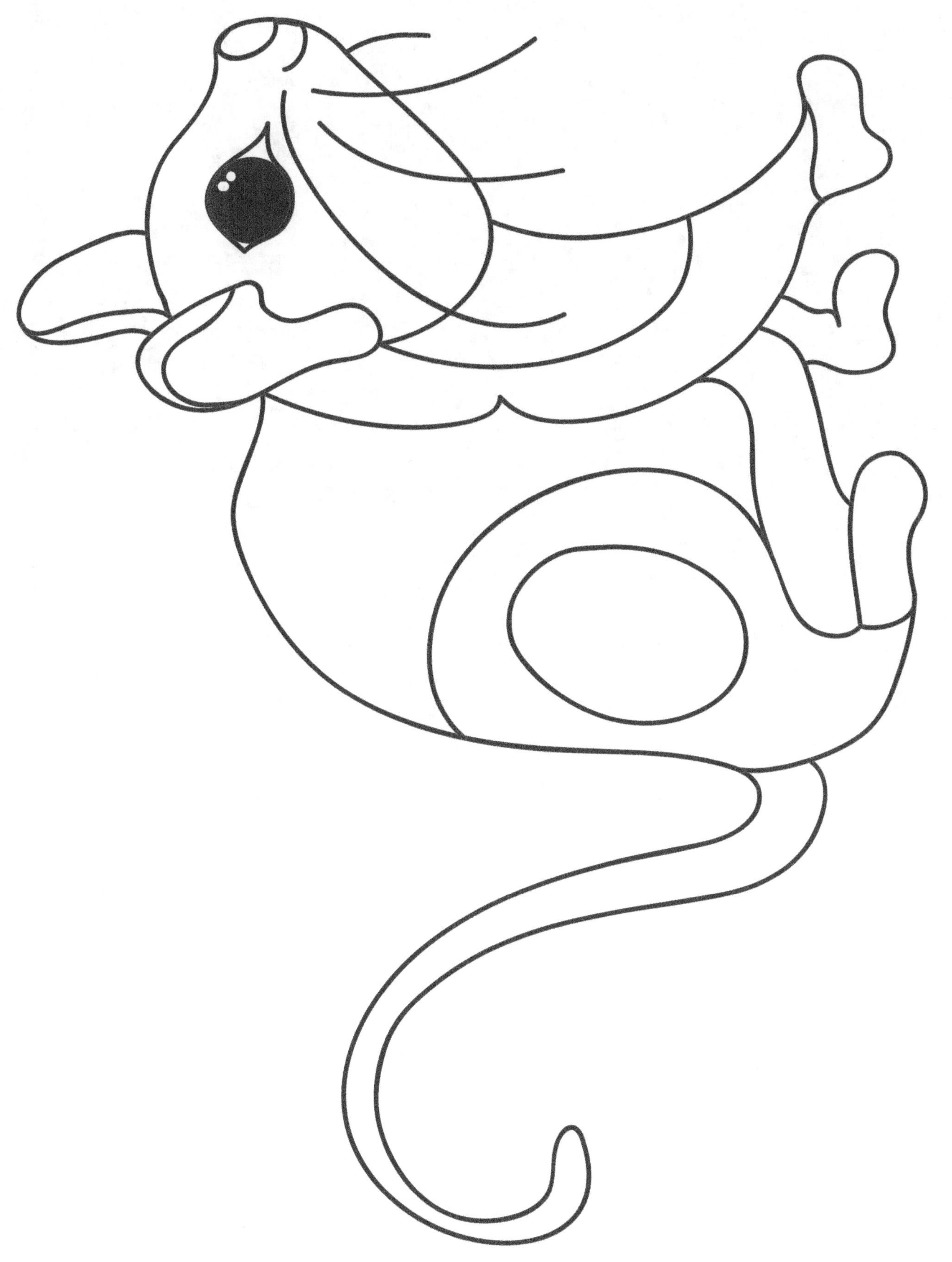

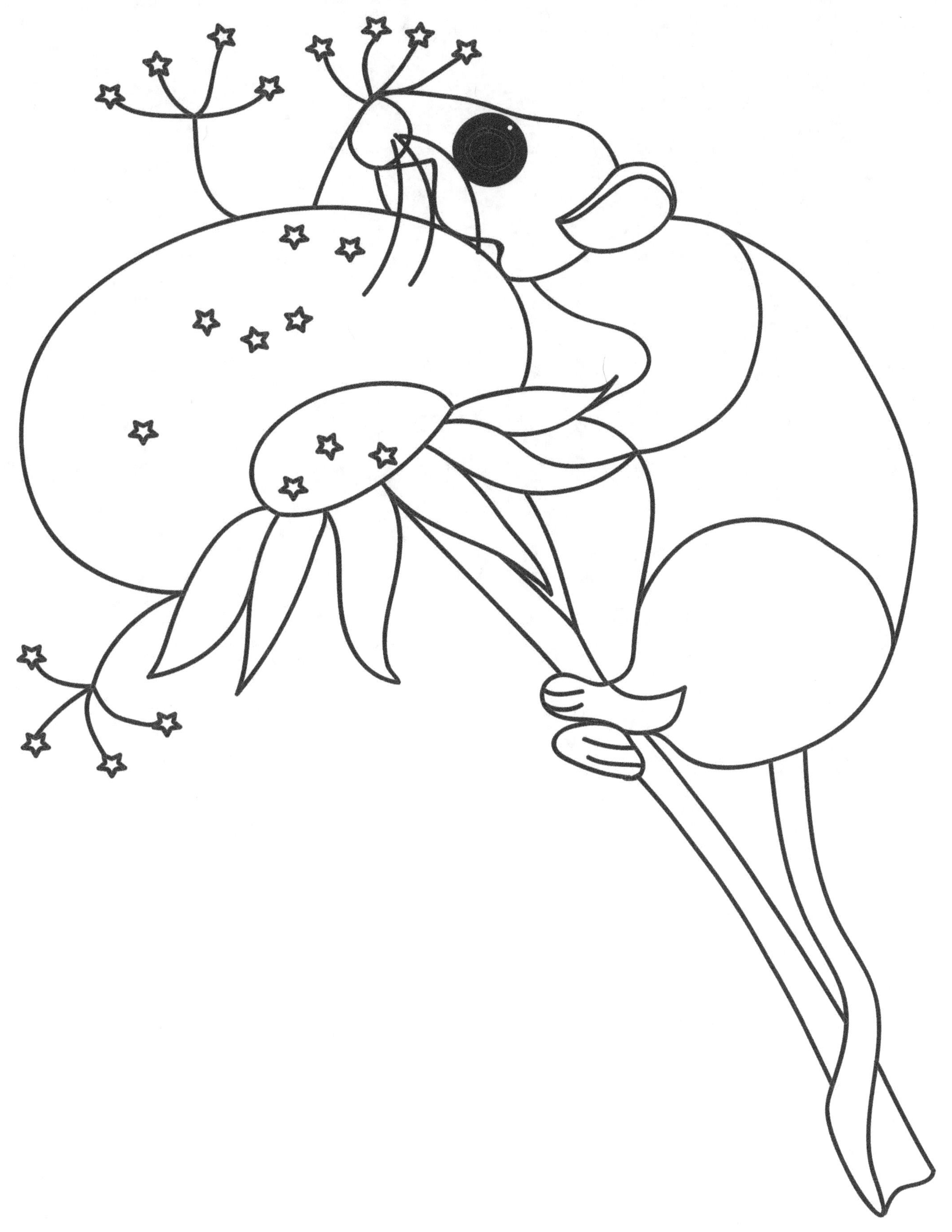

COLOR TEST PAGE

COLOR TEST PAGE

9 781986 007443